The Client Feedback Playbook

How Professional Services Firms Can
Thrive Using Client Insight

Graham Archbold

ISBN: 979 8 28160 449 9

CONTENTS

PREFACE:
THIS BOOK IS ABOUT SUSTAINABLE PROGRAMME-BUILDING – NOT QUESTION DESIGN

This book sets out the main principles and an overall approach in setting up and running a client feedback programme, whether starting from scratch or revitalising an existing one. It describes the decisions that need to be taken and best-practice approaches, without detailing every possible tactical implementation. Differences in governance and culture across firms make it impossible to prescribe a single approach.

The insights are based on first-hand experience advising the management of professional services firms since 2007, observing which ones succeed or fail and taking lessons from each. As a consultant, I've worked with dozens of leading firms across accountancy, engineering, executive search, legal and property, deploying countless online surveys and conducting more than a thousand one-to-one research interviews. Rather than detail different case studies – that don't necessarily generalise well – I've compiled the common scenarios to address the most frequent challenges you might face.

This book assumes that you are in a role that makes you responsible for client experience, be it from an operations, marketing or strategy perspective. For this reason, the emphasis is on influencing leadership colleagues, agenda setting and change management rather than the intricacies of questionnaire design or software selection, though I provide advice on these where it might be of benefit.

My own mission is to help people better understand each other; to promote listening, empathy and collaboration. Delivering feedback is a means to that because nearly all dissatisfaction with service experiences and failed commercial relationships come as a result of mismatches in expectations, derived from miscommunication; if we can fix that, we make the world a better place.

To make improvements we must identify the gaps between expectation and actual experience – too often we talk about 'quality' without the means to define or measure its many dimensions. The solution is to break experience down into its components, in the same way that manufacturers make products better and safer by understanding the minutiae of each component, then recalibrating and upgrading. Gathering feedback on these components unlocks the possibility of improvement, renewal, and growth.

This book is a guide to setting up and running a *sustainable* client feedback programme – one that succeeds and perpetuates because the outcomes it generates fuels business growth so self-evidently that to discontinue it would be as unthinkable as padlocking the front door and disconnecting the phones.

Getting it right benefits everyone – professionals and clients alike. Finding ways to improve and to implement change removes the niggles and hindrances that undermine positive commercial relationships.

CHAPTER 1
INTRODUCTION TO CLIENT FEEDBACK IN PROFESSIONAL SERVICES

True intuitive expertise is learned from prolonged experience with good feedback on mistakes.

—Daniel Kahneman

Asking for and acting on client feedback is a key tenet in most successful businesses, yet many professional services firms became successful without much more than the occasional 'fireside chat'. What got you here isn't what will get you to the next level of success, though. While feedback programmes are gaining popularity, properly structured ones are still so far from commonplace that they offer competitive advantage for those firms that do commit to action. Transitioning from ad hoc listening to ongoing programmes is crucial, as is forecasting future behaviour and linking to financial outcomes.

Client feedback is more important than ever

Expectations matter. The instant gratification of modern digital experiences means that, as consumers, we expect ever clearer communication, ever faster delivery and ever better quality.

Meanwhile the idea that business purchases occur in a purely rational, emotion-free vacuum has been thoroughly debunked. Our personal and professional experiences are cross-pollinated: what delights us as consumers becomes the baseline in business. As a result, the bar for positive client experience keeps rising.

For forward-thinking professional services firms, a key part of the solution is client feedback. Through efforts to better understand changing client needs, firms are able to deliver what's required with fewer service errors and omissions. They can also generate higher levels of satisfaction and loyalty, which lead to longer, more profitable relationships.

Some trailblazers have already moved from ad hoc feedback exercises that tick compliance boxes into rolling programmes integral to successful service delivery. Rather than simply monitoring opinion, advanced feedback programmes forecast future buying behaviour and produce practical recommendations for change and improvement in the business.

A further step is gauging cultural alignment between suppliers and clients. For example, environmental, social and governance requirements are increasingly being given serious consideration. Clients are challenging firms, demanding that claimed policies and actual practices match up. Clients want to see tangible benefits from long-promised technological innovations that are meant to be realised in cost efficiencies, not to mention the overhauling of fee and billing models.

Few firms are achieving all this but the ones that are, do so by taking a holistic view of relationships, piecing together

data from different sources and mapping out client journeys before optimising them. It means getting views from not only decision-makers but all influencers and front-line users of the firm's
services to give a rounded view of the corporate relationship.

As well as understanding the views of clients in different
job roles, recognising the key touchpoints is important too. Experience ratings will vary through the client lifecycle from
onboarding, at post-transaction, as well as at overall relationship
review, to eventual offboarding. Analysing the matrix of clients
and their experiences, enables firms to segment the client base
and so better tailor solutions to client needs.

There is also the need to be more adaptable in the channels used in capturing feedback. Whereas telephone and face-
to-face interviewing were the go-to modes of canvassing feedback from high value clientele, post-pandemic the default for
business meetings is web conference. The expectation of clients
is that feedback sessions will utilise this approach too, which is
a boon to client research because the format combines the personalisation and stimulating interaction of an in-person meeting
with the ease and convenience of a telephone call.

From 'nice-to-have' to 'always-on' business insight

While some firms have made huge strides toward becoming client-centric businesses with an 'always-on' listening function,
most professional services firms lag far behind. Nominally, they
are running some form of 'client listening', whereby once every
two or three years a handful of senior execs at client organisations are invited to take part in nice 'fireside chats', producing
reassuring reports that confirm how satisfied everyone is. These
reports get filed away and everyone agrees not to bother those
clients again because everything is fine as it is.

Funnily enough, when the same exercise is repeated a few years later, the clients will mostly be different organisations. At least half. Why is there such a lack of client retention? Why do these seemingly happy and loyal clients sack off their trusted advisors? At some point, something changed and the firm didn't find out about it. This is the problem with the gentle art of client listening employed at most firms: it's too passive and infrequent.

Voice of the Client (VoC) programmes tend to be an improvement on client listening because they are usually designed to be a constant function within the business. However, they are a separate function independent of the business operations or strategy creation, so the streams of information they generate aren't necessarily exploited by the wider business as effectively as they could be.

A far superior strategy is to introduce a client feedback programme. Or a CX (Client Experience) programme (client listening's much cooler cousin). CX is a holistic and ongoing process for converting criticism and praise into action: business change, operational improvement and occasionally, strategic overhaul.

Client listening is just the first step. The definition of a programme is 'a set of related measures or activities with a particular long-term aim'. For the 'long-term aim' you can also read 'strategy'. It's not a one-off task you tick-off as completed, it's an embedded means of achieving long-term strategic objectives. Likewise, 'feedback' implies a closed-loop system in which the input is acted upon in some way. 'Experience' is much more than the auditory; it encompasses all aspects of interactions. Experience has depth and nuance, with layers to interpret and understand.

All these terms – Listening, Voice, Programme, Feedback, Experience – may appear to be mere semantics, but words do matter. To this end, 'client listening' needs to be ditched as an end in itself. The same goes for 'voice of the client'. Instead, ambitious firms need to establish client feedback and experience programmes that are integral to service delivery, in order to learn from clients and drive business growth.

Why client feedback programmes fail (and how to avoid such doom)

Many professional services firms have sporadic client feedback programmes – some even have slightly neurotic ones. A new hire will come in, identify problems at the firm, diagnose a lack of client understanding and prescribe a feedback function as one of the solutions. They'll set about a survey of some kind, do all the hard work of getting everyone on board, extract a few valuable insights, even get some change management going and real service improvement. Then they'll move on, and that'll be it. Another one-off project completed. Ticked off. However, this implies certain assumptions: the firm will never win a new client; nobody's needs will ever change; and no new competitors will ever come along with better alternatives. Consequently, it all gets filed away – until a few years later when, another 'forward-thinker' points out that measuring and improving client experience might be a good idea.

These aren't tinpot firms staffed by plodders; this is true of many national and multi-national firms, advising major corporations on massive matters. They operate with a collective amnesia, only occasionally waking up to remember how the marketing function aids commercial success by being market-orientated.

The primary cause is down to the nature of professional services firms. Unlike in consumer goods companies, where the marketing department is central to the enterprise, most firms started out with practitioners who progressed and succeeded because of their expertise and the reputation that developed from it. Success came *despite* a lack of market research, positioning, and promotion – not because of it. The marketing function developed out of what were then – and sometimes now – are referred to as 'support staff': those people who take care of the ancillary tasks that distract from the actual fee-earning priorities. Most firms have a clear demarcation between the fee-earners and the business services folk, with the latter rarely being holders of equity in the business.

If not for the fact that HMRC has the power to fine, sanction, and ultimately close down firms that fail to file with Companies House, submit accounts, or pay taxes, then most firms would have the same approach to accounting functions as their marketing ones. Perhaps, with the exception of the accountancy firms, they'd only ever get round to totting up their finances every few years.

The sporadic and inconsistent approach to the market research function means that most feedback programmes fail within a short timeframe. This is a waste of time and resource for everyone involved, particularly clients who have had their expectations raised only to be disappointed that interest in improving service was merely a fleeting initiative.

The biggest mistake is *not creating a financial link with success*. Call it return on investment (ROI), or similar terms. Programmes that can't evidence the money saved or generated will never be viewed as an essential business process. A dollar sign attached to your work is required in order to get attention at board-level strategy and investment meetings.

The second mistake is *relying on overly manual or time-intensive processes* that sit with people who have more pressing priorities. You need people dedicated to making it happen and they in turn need to make it easy for everyone else to engage and support. If you have to make a 'request' to access clients – as opposed to having a mandate to do so – then you're on a hiding to nothing.

The third is *not having senior leadership's buy-in*. Their buy-in is not only what helps secure the resource, but is also what leads to inculcating feedback into the firm's culture. When leaders make feedback a priority, it gets incorporated into operational processes, human resource agendas, and financial appraisals.

Professional services require a different approach to B2C

The big difference between collecting feedback from business buyers compared with consumers is volume. With Business to Consumer (B2C) research, you can't hope to get feedback from all your buyers and nor do you want or need to contact them all. In B2C, sampling matters. You want a statistically representative sample from which you can extrapolate insights and apply those lessons to the whole buyer population. You address problems that are common because you know many people encounter them. It's very much a numbers game.

By contrast, in Business to Business (B2B) – and especially professional services – what matters is value (of relationships) rather than volume. The value of a client organisation in terms of revenue and profit can be tremendous. The typical Pareto principle (the 80-20 rule) usually applies with a small number of clients accounting for disproportionately high amounts of income. This means that rather than taking examples and then generalising, you focus on those most valuable client relationships.

Where you uncover problems or opportunities at a single client organisation, the tendency is to work on fixing or exploiting those at account level in order to retain the client, rather than considering whether or not those actions need to be applied more broadly, to others with a similar profile.

This requires coordinated cultural commitment to client-focus – and the organisational agility to respond. Without those elements, the programme only detracts value by taking up the client's time and raising expectations of improvement without then delivering. Given that few firms have much resource allocated to improvement, it's best to focus on clients for whom there is evidence of high lifetime value – not only has spend been high to date, but there is the prospect of that pattern continuing.

While this information can be extracted from practice management systems and predicted based on sales pipelines, complicating professional services client feedback on the B2B side is the fact that you rarely have a single buyer at the client. Oftentimes, there are a multitude of points of contact, with different roles and responsibilities, needs and preferences, and attitudes and prejudices towards your firm. Understanding the dynamics within a client organisation can be complex and difficult to map out.

Some firms will categorise the different players according to personas and survey individuals by different methods and attribute different weightings to the importance of the views they express. Accordingly, one person's complaint may be fast-tracked, while another's is acknowledged but merely added to the backlog of issues to address sometime or never.

The groupings of buyers tend to be categorised along the lines of (1) decision-maker, (2) influencer, and (3) front-line. People at the top of the buyer hierarchy will be surveyed personally via interview, while those lower down are invited to complete online surveys. This isn't necessarily the right order: you might want the C-suite to feel they're getting premium treatment, yet the operational fixes that are tricky to understand and rectify come from lower down and require more interaction. The decision as to whom should be surveyed by which method varies greatly from firm to firm.

Overall, the upshot is this: you need to invest more time and effort in selecting who to survey. This is particularly valid when surveying everyone isn't an option. You focus on the big spenders for maximum impact on your bottom line. In turn, within each client organisation, you want to identify the key points of contact and use the most appropriate survey mechanism – don't get caught up with the idea of sampling in the way that you would for B2C research.

Client research is a different beast within professional services from other B2B businesses. Anyone moving into professional services from outside the industry, even a related one like finance, tends to get a shock.

It primarily comes down to organisational structural differences and governance. Professional services firms long enjoyed (and still do to some extent) a protected status because the need to have special licensing or qualifications acts as a barrier to entry. The likes of law firms were, for most of their histories, not permitted to advertise their services. They operated under a partnership model, with shared liabilities and a relatively democratic decision-making structure. Even now, leadership at most firms consists of successful practitioners representing their fellow professionals in different functions, rather than business or subject specialists who have transitioned in from the commercial world.

All this tends to add up to steady and stable organisations that admit commercial practices only on a gradual basis; there are very few innovative 'disrupter' firms out there.

Takeaways

- Client feedback is no longer about one-off satisfaction surveying: it must monitor relationships continuously and holistically as a means of predicting future buying decisions.

- In-person and telephone canvassing is dead – long live online surveys and web-based video meetings; these are now the default methods of 'taking the pulse' of valued clients.

- To contribute to your firm's growth, go beyond 'client listening' and adopt a 'client feedback programme' type of moniker, with a focus on improving client experience.

- Your programme must establish a financial link with success, demonstrating return on investment, to move from 'nice-to-have' to being a core source of business intelligence valued by everyone.

- You need a mandate to access and approach the firm's client base as and when needed, rather than relying on individual requests that can be blocked by uncooperative or inattentive fee-earners.

- You absolutely need senior leadership's backing and a champion at the top, in order to put client feedback in the spotlight and on top of agendas across the firm.

- Feedback in professional services is different from B2C: focus on your biggest, most valuable clients – don't get caught up trying to use randomised sampling that treats all clients the same (they're not!).

CHAPTER 2
THE STRATEGIC, OPERATIONAL, AND FINANCIAL BENEFITS OF CLIENT FEEDBACK

Criticism, like rain, should be gentle enough to nourish a man's growth without destroying his roots.

—Frank A. Clark

If client feedback reaps nothing but pat-on-the-back 'nice-to-haves', you're doing it wrong. Research that reveals changing client needs and wants, the behavioural drivers behind purchase decisions and emerging market trends is what fuels excellence in service delivery. Feedback is key to diagnosing operational and strategic problems, identifying opportunities, and motivating teams to raise standards and improve performance. Moreover, the very act of giving feedback reminds clients of your successful track record together, thereby reinforcing their loyalty.

Retaining and growing good clients; offloading the undesirable ones

The absolute core objective of any client feedback programme and the benefit it delivers is retaining clients over the long-term. Especially those clients deemed most desirable – the ones the programme should prioritise and invest in the most, that represent outsized profits for the firm. Doing so reduces the need to spend time and money on winning new ones. Every year different statistics appear, quantifying the costliness of pursuing new business versus retaining old business; these figures are sometimes spurious but intuitively, we know how much easier it is dealing with long-time clients than it is prospecting strangers.

Soliciting feedback can also lead directly to new business. It can be by bringing the firm back to the front of the client's mind. Occasionally, a line of questioning highlights service lines clients previously were unfamiliar with. More often, though, it comes from the active follow-up afterwards.

Armed with an enhanced understanding of the client's needs and preferences, informal follow-up conversations – or more formal account reviews – go into areas that would never be explored otherwise. Rather than technical details of delivery, business problems and strategic challenges take centre stage. This means opportunity to introduce colleagues and services, where appropriate.

By contrast, the least talked about benefit of client feedback is how it can aid in parting company with clients that are a poor fit. Often, the majority of complaints come from clients who should never have been taken on originally, or else the firm has outgrown. These clients effectively self-identify: they're the ones with the unreasonable expectations or unfair criticisms. They're asking to be fired.

It's a brave act to offload clients, to turn down their money, but it can be for the benefit of all concerned. Often these are the clients whom nobody likes servicing – they damage employee morale and are the least profitable (they'll often prove loss-making, if the calculations can be done). They also damage your reputation by spreading negative word-of-mouth in public. It can require some soul-searching and internal debate within the firm, but learning who these clients are and terminating the commercial relationship can be hugely beneficial in the long run.

Compiling competitor intelligence

Even if you have a warm and candid supplier-buyer relationship, asking point-blank about the competition tends not to be an easy or comfortable conversation. You feel like you're prying, so it's better to stick to delivering a great service and getting along well, without the risk of causing affront. That's how most professionals feel: there's something deeply inappropriate about asking how others do things, and where your firm might be ahead or behind. It might get personal, it might reveal your flaws and – by asking – your insecurities.

Yet competitor intelligence is hugely valuable in developing and improving your services and offering. Much of the time, you can't intuitively know what's missing unless someone tells you. There is a wealth of operational and – sometimes – strategic information, that's commonplace to your client, and which is otherwise inaccessible to you, as one of the competitors in the marketplace.

This is one of the key areas where creating a separate forum outside of service delivery, a somewhat formal review exercise, establishes a setting where it's not only a suitable environment to explore comparisons with others, it's fully expected. As part of a feedback exercise, clients are not surprised to be asked about rival firms. They may decide to limit what they share but it's not damaging to the relationship to ask, provided the right approach is taken and techniques employed.

In some instances, particularly where the client is a loyal promoter, they'll be keen to supply as much intelligence as they can; they may want to remove another provider if only your firm can up its game, or demonstrate to a decision-maker that your capabilities are superior. The client may have been waiting for the opportunity to share their insights.

In other instances, the individual may be more reticent to divulge key information. They may, ostensibly, cite procurement rules that restrict what they can say about work that is carried out under confidential contracts. Whether this policy, as such, exists in writing anywhere isn't relevant; it tells you about their attitude and sentiment toward the firm. This sort of response is most common with public sector organisations. As an opening gambit, it does not for a second mean they won't give you interesting insights. However, it does mean you might have to do some coaxing and approach the subject from different angles. This is where employing a third party pays dividends. With an intermediary, there is a buffer, a safe space.

The types of information you can learn about your competition is varied. For every area of enquiry you make, there is an opportunity to ask for a comparison against others. The priority for many partners is to learn about fees and, as useful as this can be, should only be one aspect – frequently, you'll hear how the hourly rate is higher or lower by X amount – but this doesn't matter, because one party or another manages to deliver overall better value, care of *how* the service is actually delivered. Learning these differences can be much more practically useful than knowing agreed rates are at a ten per cent discount or premium.

Simply uncovering the identity of competitors can be a revelation. Indeed, learning that there *are* competitors, despite the relationship partner having insisted there is an exclusive trusted advisor arrangement, can be illuminating! Knowing which other firms serve the client, understanding the basket of comparison, is a great starting point and a lever in developing the relationship. For example, being able to exploit a competitor's limitations in terms of geographical reach, specialism, or cost-base. Many aspects of service that you are told make another firm special, or the reason they are retained despite other drawbacks, prove to be easily matched or surpassed from your perspective, whereas the client is under the misconception that they are offering a unique differentiator.

Lessons can be uncovered as to how the relationship is managed, how advice or documentation is delivered, how pricing mechanisms work, what added value initiatives are on offer – you can learn how to match and beat the competition where it matters the most. Usually, you just need to ask.

Revealing otherwise unknown threats and opportunities

Competitor intelligence is one key source of otherwise hidden opportunities. There are many other unknowns that surveying can reveal. A simple one, for instance, is what clients think you *actually* do and offer as a business.

As practitioners within the firm, it's impossible to unlearn everything you know from the inside, and see the firm from an outsider's perspective. You may think your offering is clear: after all, you have these service lines for these particular market sectors. Maybe your firm specialises in something particular; you're the best of the best, and have the industry awards to prove it. But ask a typical client, and their interpretation will sound as though it's been arrived at via a pretty inattentive round of Chinese whispers. They'll recall the main thing they use your firm for, but then anything else that's stuck will be minimal, slightly vague, or completely inaccurate.

This will often lead to some surprise and disbelief within the firm. How can they have been using you for the last ten years and not know that you have an [insert team or practice name here], when those experts sit next to the client relationship partner? How have they missed all those mailshots? Didn't they notice you sponsored that event they were at last month?

As frustrating as the lessons might be, client research will tell you which parts of your marketing messages have landed and which have sailed wide of the mark. Finding out what the client does and doesn't know about your offering helps you to fine-tune your marketing messages and choice of channels.

This is helpful for marketing, but also – more directly – in sales. While awareness of services is likely a longer-term objective to set and work towards, at an individual account level there is often an immediate opportunity to cross-sell services. For example, you might learn the client is using a competitor, whom they acknowledge is inferior, for a service you offer. Or, there's been a change of strategy at corporate level, which means departmental priorities have changed and there's expansion planned, requiring different supplier resources. Whatever the development, a simple follow-up activity is an introduction to someone in the relevant department from your firm. Nothing complex, and often an outcome that pays off quickly, simply because the timing was right.

Similarly, feedback can be used to inform and win bids in a direct manner. Collecting feedback six months to a year out from a client's upcoming procurement exercise allows time to address weaknesses. Service failures can be addressed, resources added, and unmet needs discovered. Undertaking feedback well ahead of a pitch, you can literally ask the client how they want your proposal and presentation to be in a relatively subtle manner. That's not the case if you try to ask two weeks before. In many cases, you either can't solicit feedback once procurement professionals are involved, or else any response has to be shared among all the firms vying for appointment, thus removing the possibility of obtaining competitive advantage.

One of the biggest threats to ameliorate is not knowing that an individual is dissatisfied with the service you're delivering and unwilling to undertake the confrontation required to tell you. That's not always directly: it can be that Contact A informs you that Contact B is unhappy or planning something that will remove you from the picture. A survey or interview offers an easy and appropriate forum in which you can glean some home truths.

Making operational and strategic improvements

Client feedback will tell you – directly and indirectly – where and how to make business improvements at two levels: operations and strategy. Together, they enable you to reap financial rewards.

Individual clients will relay to you where service is below expectations; formulate your questions right and they'll also explain what needs to change. There are many means of doing this: asking clients to rank service elements in order of importance or preference; asking trade-off questions that force choices between options A and B; finding ways to help your client think through their needs and preferences. This sort of work can lead not only to improvements but huge cost-savings too. After surveying your client base, you may learn that clients don't actually like or appreciate parts of your service that you mistakenly thought of as value-adds. Meanwhile, another cheap and cheerful giveaway is the thing that's kept them coming back year after year. You'd never know this unless you asked.

Many of the little niggles that irritate clients are things that can be fixed in no time at all. Other improvements might be costly and have a long lead time, but at least (by having consulted your clients) you now know which matter most and can correctly prioritise them.

Beyond the day-to-day, client feedback should be a source of insight that feeds into and helps direct strategic decision-making and objective-setting. It works in a range of ways. At an elementary level, there's a gauge of satisfaction which indicates if clients are happy with the service they're receiving; a simple feedback loop. There are patterns that are easy to spot, like when a practice is below par or a particular stage in the customer journey sees a drop-off in satisfaction.

The aggregation of many points of view, combined with demographic and financial data goes deeper – it tells you which particular client segments are most or least satisfied. Or which have differing needs and preferences. From this, you can learn which type of client is easiest to satisfy, and lean into them. Likewise, you may choose to withdraw from targeting those for whom your service or particular methods of delivering don't work. It's not always immediately apparent that a selection of dissatisfied clients has any similar traits: you need to triangulate, bringing together data from different sources – but when the evidence is in, it becomes easy to see, and the business case makes itself.

Client feedback helps train your eye on the horizon. By tracking information year on year, you get an early warning of change ahead in needs and expectations. For example, performance scores start to decline for a certain service performance attribute or service line. Here, it could be that ratings for availability of the professional are declining each quarter, suggesting overstretched teams. Or perhaps the tax team is registering historically poor satisfaction scores. Informal or anecdotal feedback along the lines of 'such and such is hard to get hold of' might not have made this obvious but when the scores start to stack up, the evidence is there. This sort of data, visualised on a dashboard, flashes a warning light, which may need to be corroborated against other sources, but mustn't be ignored.

Headline metrics like CSAT, CES, and particularly NPS, have all been shown to be effective predictors of future buying behaviour, and therefore sales revenues. Client feedback sentiment tends to lead changes in behaviour: when ratings from a particular client go from stellar to middling, then it won't be a surprise when the note comes a few months later, telling you that the procurement folk have reminded your contacts that your contract is long overdue review and it's time to run a competitive tender. They might try to reassure you that it's all routine. But what if you'd acted as soon as you knew about the initial deterioration in scores?

Acting on feedback and any sign of less than complete engagement – not just outright complaints – avoids bean-counting and beauty parades, in turn saving costs and important client relationships.

Enhancing the firm's culture and brand

How can any firm claim to be client-focused, yet have no structured and operational mechanism for gathering feedback and actioning changes? We can talk about how having a client feedback programme improves your firm's brand, but underlying this is simply having integrity: delivering on what you promise.

Anyone can claim to listen to clients but unless there is a person who undertakes it, using particular and consistent means, and is held accountable to make it visible to others and used within the business, then the claim is fraudulent.

A client feedback programme aids a firm's brand internally among employees by helping rally people together around a central purpose. It prevents a 'them and us' attitude where everyone's job would be much easier if not for clients making unreasonable demands.

Sharing praise and compliments that come directly from clients raises pride in one's work, and boosts the morale of teams that pull together to deliver. Too often, and especially for non-client-facing employees, without a client feedback programme there is a disconnect between work and outcomes. Everyone needs recognition of their work, to actually hear from the people who benefit from their efforts, to know that what they do is worthwhile, and that people benefit at a human level from their efforts.

Hearing praise and receiving a simple 'thank you' can be a million times more rewarding emotionally than financial compensation can ever be. At a time when employee wellbeing is high on executive agendas, here is an easy way to improve mental welfare. In this way, feedback develops your firm's culture, its integrity, and its purpose.

The programme does much the same externally too. It evidences claims of client-centricity; it showcases your firm as culturally caring and progressive. The feedback in the form of testimonials (where permission has been sought to use comments externally) is valuable as promotional collateral. Rather than the firm boasting, clients corroborate claims with examples of their own experience. As compared to talking about expertise and track record in the industry, actual client experience is both a more subtle and more effective form of marketing. Increasingly, headline benchmarks like the Net Promoter Score are recognised and understood by prospective clients.

Beyond surface-level positive associations, client feedback programmes boost brand affinity. In taking part in the firm's research fieldwork, clients become involved in the firm's cause. It educates them about the firm's values, and the act of participation makes them a part of the team – no longer a passive recipient of services but an active co-creator. It's one thing to watch from the sidelines; quite another to join the field of play. When people play a role in your success, they become fans, ambassadors, partners. The best firms use client feedback as a means to brand differentiation and loyalty.

Innovation in developing new products and services

Client feedback isn't solely a source of critique of current services; approached correctly, it gives you the starting point for creating entirely new products and services from scratch.

By stepping outside your own service delivery methods and asking about wider business pain-points and challenges, clients will articulate unmet needs which they don't necessarily realise have potential solutions.

It's that old Henry Ford thing: if you'd asked customers, they'd have said they wanted a faster horse. On the face of it, the meaning seems to be that market research can't help with breakthroughs in service because clients don't know what they don't know. However, they can – and will – talk about frustrations and drawbacks they currently experience if you ask them to walk you through their current steps in fulfilling their needs. It's your job to then understand their experience, their journey, imagine alternatives, and create those step-change solutions that wipe the floor with previous methods.

Often, it entails starting with unpicking niggles, exploring what your competitors offer (as well as others from different industries) and then posing hypothetical questions to get the imagination firing. Collecting the outputs and combining them with the feelings expressed and ideas generated by other clients, gives you valuable material to work with internally, in reconstructing services or designing new ones.

It can prove to be that you already have the right elements; they simply need to be repackaged as a singular product that is easier to understand and purchase from you. You know how your service works and what the benefits are, but for an outsider it needs to be clearly structured. Making a service available and readily accessible seems obvious, but is often overlooked.

Reinforcing loyalty to the firm

Above and beyond all the other benefits of client listening (even if you ask less than perfect questions, overlook opportunities and miss out on competitor intelligence), the very act of asking for feedback strengthens relationships. That's even with people who don't respond when they see a 'You Said, We Did' type of report; they now know you are listening: 'I didn't have time to give them my feedback but at least they asked me. When I do have something to share then I'll make the effort because I know they'll do something with it.'

Listening to your client shouldn't just be a promotional marketing exercise but it does have that effect. It's another channel of communication; another subtle reminder that you're there for them. A post-transaction review rounds off a matter, confirming that it's been dealt with and seals the matter with a sense of closure. With an annual service review, it might have been months since you've been in touch working on a live project but here it is, a little reminder of the success you had together on that matter earlier in the year.

And this is key: the act of revisiting positive experiences brings them front of mind and reminds the person just how much they enjoyed working together, how great the outcome made them look in front of colleagues, how it led to progression in their career. It calls to mind that bonus they received – or whatever outcome came about – that you may have been completely unaware of at the time. It resurfaces positive emotion.

In effect, with a happy client, you spend the duration of the feedback interaction with them regaling all the reasons they made the right choice in selecting you in the first place and reminding themselves why they should use you again in future. Psychologically, this is the client selling to themselves. You can't spend an hour giving feedback on a service provider, telling the interviewer how much you like them and how they're the best in the market, without subtly convincing yourself to continue using them. The fact that you've invested time means that you are committing yourself to the firm again in the future. Otherwise, why would you waste your time in trying to help?

Takeaways

- The main benefit of a client feedback programme is in retaining and growing desirable client relationships while offloading the toxic or unprofitable ones.

- Feedback exercises produce a wealth of competitor intelligence, especially when an independent third-party is deployed.

- Collecting feedback is a key means of identifying opportunities and threats to the relationship that otherwise might not become apparent in day-to-day account servicing.

- Client feedback directs you to all of the operational fixes required to retain and grow relationships which, at an aggregated level, inform strategy decisions too.

- Client feedback is a motivator for teams and individuals who seldom have direct client interaction or receive explicit praise.

- By involving clients in the future development of the firm, they become brand ambassadors with a stake in your cause, motivated to help you make improvements.

- Listen well and clients will express their frustrations and unmet needs. You can explore and formulate solutions to these, creating entirely new products and services.

- The act of giving feedback reminds clients of the successful outcomes you achieved for them and reinforces their loyalty to the firm.

CHAPTER 3
GETTING BUY-IN FROM THE FIRM'S KEY STAKEHOLDERS

Behaviour precedes belief – that is, most people must engage in a behaviour before they accept that it is beneficial; then they see the results, and then they believe that it is the right thing to do ...implementation precedes buy-in; it does not follow it.

—Douglas B. Reeves

The catch-22 to getting off the ground is that you need senior stakeholders who'll advocate and be ambassadors but to attract them, you need evidence demonstrating it won't blow up in their faces. A small-scale pilot picking up quick-win benefits is one means, as is proving the economic value by calculating prospective return on investment. Early on, what pays dividends is rather than obsessing over satisfaction scores, instead focusing on fostering a feedback culture and experiencing the benefits.

Get leadership on board but be selective about your champions

You need the big guns on board right from the start. Having your CEO or managing partner set out a strategic plan that prioritises the understanding, measuring and improving of client experience, immediately gets your client feedback programme on everyone's agenda. Stressing the importance to others, saying 'this is our way of doing things; this is part of our culture; I want everyone behind this' makes a tremendous difference. There's having buy-in from leadership, and there's having it *driven* by leadership. The latter doesn't guarantee success but it certainly gives you a leg up.

In reality, this isn't always how it works. The chances are that leadership will be open to such a programme but it will be only one of many initiatives sitting in their inbox. You'll need to spell out the importance by showing them the benefits and making the programme easy to implement.

In some circumstances, and especially at the early stages, it can actually be better if the programme is *not* top leadership's pet project. This is because it removes dependencies on the time and attention of someone who may find themselves caught up in any number of other important projects. In those circumstances, having their backing, rather than their leadership, is a good thing.

If not your chief executive or managing partner, another member of senior leadership may well be a better bet as your programme sponsor or champion. The characteristics you're looking for are someone who is already established and credible within the firm, someone who isn't putting themselves at risk, and isn't scared of being exposed or embarrassed by any bumps in the road you might encounter. We're talking confident and ambitious. Often, that is someone who is a future managing partner who will benefit from association with an eye-catching initiative that puts them more closely in touch with the client base, with increased operational involvement and in a position to champion change.

They need to be someone who will carve out time and be committed to action, not just a motivational cheerleader. For this reason, another type of character who may be a good fit is an experienced practitioner who is stepping back from fee-earning work and wants a broader role in the business. They will have held important roles in the firm in the past, are well networked internally, and carry a good deal of gravitas. This person knows how the organisation works, the internal politics and personalities and, consequently, how to make things happen.

It's this person you should work with to tie the programme into the firm's strategy, ensuring that it contributes to specific aims and objectives. Where possible, you'll quantify the impact you're aiming to have: X percentage improvement over Y timeframe. You'll develop your plan to get further engagement and buy-in from others within the firm's leadership.

And while we're talking about a single champion, it stands to reason that the larger your firm, the greater the advantage of having more than one. The more involved key individuals are at the outset in designing and scoping the programme, the more they will be committed to leading from the front when it comes to communication and wider roll-out.

There are a number of techniques for getting the leadership alignment needed. The best way to do it is to run a pilot of the programme on a small scale within a small part of the business, demonstrate how it works and what the benefits will be, building a business case around it. This mini-programme will be used to demonstrate, end-to-end, how issues will be identified and dealt with, and to illustrate how the firm benefits.

Doing this helps you spot any likely barriers that will appear elsewhere so you know what you'll face and can plan ahead. For instance, it could be an issue with your CRM system around data quality that makes you realise you'll need more resource or to allow more time for compiling target respondent names. It'll show you what questions resonate best with which participants. Working out the processes, you'll compile your own how-to and set of FAQs that, going forward, will help.

Ideally, you're going to uncover an account that is saved as a result, or an opportunity that wouldn't have otherwise been recognised and which demonstrates a great return on investment from this sort of client listening. It may even be relatively modest improvements that can be made or especially good news testimonials.

These sorts of show-and-tell wins demonstrate the benefits in a tangible real-world way. You get to see a complete cycle of issue identification, how you go about getting to a resolution, the business benefit, and the client's reaction (primarily emotional but hopefully financial too).

If you're able to uncover some surprising insights that might not be the full picture but invite a desire to explore and discover if they are part of a wider phenomenon, that will be an aid too. The stronger the story behind your findings and the more emotion, the better your case. That's not to say that the financial argument isn't also very important too.

Calculate prospective return on investment

It's the same as with most new initiatives in business – if you can, then SHOW THEM THE MONEY! We instinctively know that improving client experience will pay big returns, but to secure investment you need a more precision-engineered case.

There are lots of publicly available statistics to be found via the likes of the Harvard Business Review and other business publications that emphasise how leaders in client experience outperform the market. Better still, though, is if you can manage to get your pilot completed and use your own data. Failing that – if you need to make the argument prior to the pilot – it can be done without the implemented change, just on more of a hypothetical basis. You want to calculate the value of your specific programme and retaining clients by working out the value of current clients, as well as the cost of winning new ones, to make it a no-brainer to invest (it's never a cost, it's an *investment*).

Start by determining the client lifetime value (CLV) of a basket of typical clients. You probably want a number between 10 and 100 clients depending on if you are starting out focused on high value clients only or the firm's whole client base. It might be, say, on average, a spend with you of £100,000 per client.

Next, identify where you have had a known problem – either care of feedback from your pilot, or one that's otherwise come to management's attention via another means, such as a formal complaint. For example, it might be an inaccuracy in billing because fee-earners don't follow a particular procedure. For every person who has flagged it as an issue, you can assume a number are likewise displeased but haven't made it known to you. Is it likely to be experienced by 20 per cent of your clients?

Now work out your likely client churn if the problem were to go unrecognised and unrectified. Billing can be a niggly annoyance or a toys-out-the-pram matter, depending on the overall relationship health. Even assuming a mere 10 per cent of clients leave to go to a competitor, at £100,000 of CLV revenue each, it's a no-brainer to save £500,000 in churn compared to the relatively small sum of investment needed for your client feedback programme.

- 2,000 active clients over the last 12 months
- Average retention period with the firm is 5 years
- 20% experience a problem with billing (400 clients)
- Half (200) will defect if problems are not addressed
- 200 clients with a £100,000 CLV are at risk
- Identifying and addressing the billing problem is worth £20m

Even this basic approach carries so much potential that most members of leadership will want to fund further efforts. Finding problems quickly, especially ones that have quick fixes, makes the need for a programme urgent, important and easy. And this is just based on a small sample with a narrow scope in terms of issues to remedy. The return on investment is clearly even greater when factoring in contributions to winning additional work from current clients.

Set a clear purpose and achievable objectives

Too often the idea of gathering 'feedback' comes with gloomy connotations – it's accompanied by the phrase 'constructive criticism' which – euphemistically – means 'getting a kicking'. To get taken up as an initiative, the positioning should lean into the positives. How do we go from being very good to exceptional? From average to elite? You need to communicate that this will be a journey of celebrating those individuals who go the extra mile in delivering an experience that delights clients. You need to articulate a vision wherein feedback is the firm's engine of growth, helping everyone understand what is valuable and what is possible, uncovering best practices, acknowledging exceptional effort, and celebrating client successes.

To begin with, any goals or objectives you set should not involve performance targets in terms of service, satisfaction or loyalty levels you'll achieve. Instead, it should be about how effectively you can embed the culture and necessary processes that underpin an always-on programme of client feedback that makes the firm genuinely client-centric.

Clear and achievable short-term objectives would be along the lines of the number of clients surveyed. For example, '*this* percentage of the client base will be invited to take part in our relationship survey or interview process within *this* set period of time'. The short-term should all be about initial engagement and establishing the muscle memory of consistently asking for feedback.

Next might be setting a reasonable turnaround time for acknowledging, and then acting upon, feedback. It need not be too ambitious to begin with – weeks rather than days or hours – but you do need to state your intention and share it widely if you want to reach that state where everyone is agreed that 'gathering feedback is just how we do things here'.

If the firm has a stated mission, then tie the purpose of your feedback programme to that mission. If you can, come up with a snappy mantra of some sort, such as 'Our firm believes in feedback first' or 'We don't fear feedback' – you are sure to come up with something snappier. This kind of slogan, often repeated, becomes part of the culture. Indeed, giving the programme a name that's unique to the firm helps too – a play on the idea of marginal gains, being future-ready, or superior in some way – helps find a space in people's minds. Just avoid anything dull or convoluted, that sounds like it was designed by a large committee.

As your programme matures, your success factors may evolve and become more nuanced but to begin with, simple 'where are we now?' objectives work best.

Wherever possible the programme should directly support the firm's strategic plans, brand positioning, and overall culture. It's important that it is operationally critical to the business, not a siloed function that some lone individual in the business development team is responsible for and no one else.

Spreading the word throughout the firm

Before the full launch you should get everyone aware of the programme, what it's setting out to achieve, how it will work, how they'll benefit, and exactly what will be expected of them. If resource allows, there should be a proper, scheduled, internal communications campaign that ensures focus is regular and appropriately cascaded throughout the firm, so that everyone understands the relevance of their own role.

You want a short presentation to reach as wide an audience as possible, for example, at the partners' conference, the firm's AGM, or another all-hands type of event. If possible, a recorded version for sharing with anyone who doesn't attend will help you mop up the rest in terms of communications. Your content should be focused on the benefits and assuaging the common fears and objections, rather than the operational nitty-gritty.

Make sure you're not the only one banging the drum either – get anyone else presenting up to speed in advance, and help them to seed references. Your managing partner should reveal his or her enthusiasm for it; your IT director mentions how you've got systems in place; and the finance director will, of course, be looking forward to identifying any areas of unnecessary spend that can be cut!

You want your sponsors and champions on side and ready to jump in to help with anything that comes up in the Q&A at the end.

Beside this event, you'll want to raise the programme's profile through all of your usual communication channels: intranets, blogs, videos, and other literature. If you have noticeboards – physical or digital – around the office, get the message up there. Initially, this will be about setting expectations and raising awareness. Celebrating success and culturally embedding feedback will come later. You might set up a Teams or Slack channel dedicated to sharing feedback. You might have a monthly award, with a prize for making an extra effort to get client input, responding to it, or receiving special praise.

Different levers work more effectively with some individuals than others, so using varied communication channels and experimenting with different incentives increases your chances of success.

Getting help from colleagues

The bigger your firm, the less likely you'll be able to do this alone. A lot of what you need in terms of data will be in different systems, for which colleagues in different departments will be responsible.

Your task of identifying who it is you should be surveying or interviewing will typically involve extracting client records from CRM, practice management systems, or financial records. If you're really unlucky, it will need to come from individual fee-earners' Outlook contact lists (plenty of big firms have sophisticated systems but don't use them in practice).

This means that you'll need to be adaptable and well-networked within the firm to get an array of people involved and supportive. At the bare minimum you'll want a somewhat manual export of records at a set frequency, or according to a certain spend threshold. Better still, create an automated connection between your client database and your client feedback software or platform, removing the need for manual uploads and improving data accuracy.

All this assumes you have pristine up-to-date data records and that there will be no objection to providing you with it. Firms do get there; you can get there. But the reality is that, in starting out, it will be time-consuming and frustrating. Fields will be missing, and data will be inaccurate or out of date.

For this reason, the more resource you have in terms of people in your team who can coordinate, chase and action, the better. Ideally, you want people dedicated to this sort of task; it rarely works if all you have is a solitary business development person who is normally doing something else (bids, for example) and is only able to lend time to the programme ad hoc.

Even if you do have plenty of resource in your own team, do get IT onside early – even if you don't know whether you'll need them or not. Your IT guru may need time to work out how to connect different systems and platforms, whether that's for compiling lists of target respondents initially, or later adding feedback outputs back into the appropriate client records, along with relevant financial information.

The sooner you give them the heads-up the better, albeit you don't want to create an IT project out of it. Client feedback programmes die when they become IT projects, so keep the likes of actual survey mechanisms separate rather than add another project – the off-the-shelf survey solutions are made to do just what you'll need, so it's not worthwhile to try and build the application yourself.

Getting help from external consultants

Having assessed your internal resource and got a sense of how much support you'll have from other teams and departments, you will be in a position to decide what you need from external providers.

Your main decision will be whether you run most elements internally and select a survey software provider, or you engage a research partner. The software providers will dish out licences that give you and your team access to a suite of tools that enable you to design, administer, and report back on surveys.

Going the DIY route can entail a steep learning curve, requiring a lot of expertise but, more importantly, it removes the element of impartiality from the process and demands more of your time. It *can* work if you have the expertise in-house but recruiting someone in may prove more expensive than using an external party.

By partnering with an experienced research company, you free yourself up to focus on how to improve the client experience and work at a strategy level rather than getting bogged down with tactical roadblocks and having to offer technical support to the rest of the business. A research partner should get you underway quickly and leave you to represent the voice of the client within the firm.

The independence element is worth thinking hard about too, especially if your feedback programme employs personal interviews. Having an intermediary acting on behalf of the firm encourages candid feedback. It's often much easier to convey criticism (and sometimes praise too) when there's an impartial party involved who is clearly not going to be offended or try to make a defence case.

Additionally, a third party should draw on their experience in many different scenarios when it comes to acting on feedback, being able to accelerate your programme and provide value-adds such as industry benchmarking intelligence.

As frustrating as it may be, you may find that an outside consultant is sometimes given that little bit extra attention, care of their perceived objectivity, even when conveying the exact same message you would have delivered. Notwithstanding this, a good research partner will still manage to ensure that you, as their client, remain the hero behind the whole client experience initiative.

Dealing with common objections

You may face a lot of objections in the beginning – less so in relation to the principle, and more so around getting things moving in practice. It tends to be a sort of nimbyism that is commonplace in professional services – 'Yes, we should of course do that but I'm too busy and besides, I know *my* clients so well I wouldn't need to ask for feedback'.

Sometimes this sort of reaction is because the individual has never seen a really successful feedback programme in action, and so can't conceive of how they will benefit. In fact, they may be scared by poor efforts in the past that proved counterproductive. You're usually dealing with super-bright individuals, so it's not that they don't 'get it' – rather, they can choose not to get on board. The following are the most common objections and how you can go about dealing with them.

Objection 1: Clients are too busy to take part

That old chestnut. It's an understandable one; everybody everywhere seems to be overwhelmed all the time. And yet, when something is worth doing, we manage to *make* the time for it.

We're not reviewing a cheap eBay purchase here – clients invest considerable time and money in your services, and it is a basic courtesy to offer the opportunity to improve that service they are paying to get. This is in their own self-interest.

They are intelligent adults, usually senior business executives; the invitation to participate will be politely worded and easy to respond to, and likewise easy to decline politely and without the need to offer excuses. If they really are busy, behaviour will communicate that – they won't respond at all. And if the timing isn't right – for example, they're in the midst of a crisis – then it's a matter of temporarily postponing the invitation, rather than needing to rule it out altogether.

Objection 2: We already know what clients think

The professional is so close to the client, they already tell them when they're unhappy, and so there's nothing to learn. This objection is especially common from star performers who maintain a solid client portfolio, bill generously, and are simultaneously ultra-protective of their hard-won lucrative relationships. In their view, they have little to gain and, by participating, open up the risk that your efforts will only undermine the status quo.

The best approach here is charm. Appeal to their ego. They're outperforming everyone else and so we want to model their approach and methods to bring others up to their standards. The best practices that will come from sharing will demonstrate their expertise. In this way, the most resistant individuals can be converted into champions by asking them to be role models for others in the firm.

Objection 3: The feedback will only highlight problems – ones that can't be fixed

Many professionals are well qualified at identifying potential risks. For many, when times are good and there is plenty of work to be had, so what if clients are unhappy when there'll be another along to replace them anyway? This is an anti-growth mindset, fixed on churning out work, missing the bigger picture, and ultimately resulting in unnecessary client churn.

Insecure fee-earners fear getting beaten up about fees but rarely does feedback centre on price. More often, participants make a throwaway remark about it. A well-designed survey or expertly conducted interview lets the participant get complaints off their chest but also brings them around to constructive and collaborative thinking so that they help work on proposing what would constitute an improvement. Where rates come up, the discussion tends to be around the nuances of value, expectation management and communication, not price as such. As a result, the fee-earner doesn't just get a list of complaints – the solutions will be there in the answers too, perhaps not fully formed but the kernel at least.

People with these sorts of objections need to see case studies of closed-loop feedback that has paid off already. You want your feedback champions to engage them and share their stories. It's about demonstrating how feedback is in fact overwhelmingly positive and usually simple to act upon. Find case study examples that will best resonate with the individual.

You should also provide reassurance around the degree of confidentiality that will be maintained. Although client team sharing will be encouraged, wider dissemination will be contingent on the messages the feedback contains. If they retain a veto on sharing, they have the sense of retaining control and safety.

Objection 4: We've already asked for a testimonial (or directory submission)

An annoying one, but also the easiest to handle, is when there's been a recent request for some sort of contribution already.

Again, this one is a matter of timing. If it was in the last six weeks, postpone until there's been a reasonable lag. However, you do need to make the point to both the fee-earner and the end-client that this is a distinctly different exercise. Whereas the testimonial was for promotional purposes and designed to be shared publicly, this is an operational undertaking about organisational learning and continuous improvement – you're looking for opportunities to improve, not a pat on the back. The participant will see improvement to the service they receive as a result. This sort of explanation should leave no room for conflating the two different sorts of exercise.

The three most common reasons why programmes fail

Confident with our programme – with appropriate rebuttals in hand for every objection to taking part – why then do things go wrong?

At most firms you won't actually be *starting* a feedback programme. Rather, you'll be *restarting* one that had been in place in some other form but which fizzled out. You'll hear the occasional: 'Oh yes, we did a survey a couple of years ago' (check and you'll find it's been closer to 10). Nobody exactly remembers what happened – it was a one-off, clients said some jolly nice things but it's a mystery why it isn't live today.

In fact, there are just three common reasons that account for the majority of programme failures and understanding these will help guard against them. If you want to embed client feedback in the firm as a long-term core tenet of the business and leave a legacy, then plan for (and avoid) these problems.

Programmes fail when they have no clear ownership and accountability

The paradox is that you want to create a sense of ownership throughout the business, in which everyone feels they have a role, knows their contribution, and takes ownership of responsibilities. You want that culturally, but to achieve it you need an effective governance model wherein individuals are held accountable. There should be job descriptions, success criteria, and accountability in place.

You must define who will keep everyone focused on client loyalty and financial outcomes, as well as who is responsible for acting on the findings and driving accountability across teams, down to an individual level. This element of coordination is important to prevent breakdown into siloes – especially the case when operating globally or with a number of distinct business units.

Programmes fail when too little change results from the client feedback collected

Too often, feedback programmes are conducted using academic research methodologies, and the result is accurately sampled, correctly administered studies, written up in impressive language. The outputs are very 'interesting' but no one has any idea what to do with them. Either the reporting is impenetrable because of a focus on sampling methods and robust statistical techniques, or else the questions asked didn't get to the commercial imperatives of client needs, and so the observations are bland and irrelevant.

A similar trap is when interviews are conducted in an overly gentle manner, avoiding the commercial elements for fear of causing trouble. 'Fireside chats' can be lovely but if they lack incisive questioning about fees and probing questions that gather competitor intelligence, then there is nothing to action as a result.

The remedy is to ensure your research is commercially focused, not the academic sort. The standard by which you judge feedback collection should be the number and usefulness of the action points that emerge – at account, team and firm-wide level. This is a commercial, operational approach under which you understand which client data and internal processes will create change throughout the firm and enable strategic objectives to be achieved.

Programmes fail when they lack visibility across the firm

Some programmes are undertaken as covert operations, as though only senior management has the maturity and nous to handle harsh realities. This may be because of a culture of command and control or it may be out of fear of spreading negativity that might be demotivating if all the firm's failings are exposed. It's true that some feedback should be dealt with carefully. When an individual is criticised personally, perhaps unfairly, it makes sense to deal with that discreetly without wider sharing. The key is to have a safety mechanism built in so that there is a straightforward approval process that flags anything sensitive.

Overall, getting insights shared widely is key. Everyone must receive data wherever it is relevant to them, have the tools and training to understand it, and know their role in closing the loop. At the wider level, feedback statistics and key quotes should be widely available: on extranets, performance reports, and across all communication channels as universally as possible.

Takeaways

- Find a champion who will push the agenda within the firm – someone well networked, and with the time and energy to commit. Work together on securing backing from others in leadership and raising the programme's profile.

- Run a pilot – a taster of what a wider feedback programme could do. You'll get tangible examples of the benefits which you can use to justify wider roll-out.

- Calculate return on investment by working out client life-time-value and estimating how much lost revenue results from *not* fixing client problems.

- Instead of setting high levels of client satisfaction as your objective, begin by focusing on a culture of welcoming feedback – incentivise and celebrate the process itself.

- Promote the start of the programme as though you were launching a new product – it needs a campaign with backing and visibility.

- Don't do it alone: get colleagues on board to support – internally (from the likes of IT and Finance), but from an external research partner too.

- Prepare your responses to common objections – 'too busy', 'know them well', 'can't change anything', 'asked for something else' – and be ready to bat them off.

- Understand the three most common reasons why feedback programmes fail: lack of ownership and accountability; too little change management resource to fix problems; and lack of visibility and buy-in across the firm.

CHAPTER 4
CHOOSING THE RIGHT RESEARCH APPROACH AND METHODS

What is research but a blind date with knowledge?

—Will Harvey

Academics get tied up in knots over methodological approaches and best practices, but this is commercial research: we're concerned with financial outcomes – we want insights that increase revenues and profitability. Our methods, metrics and sampling all need to be justifiable in the boardroom, and especially when the CFO's red pen is ready to strike. At the same time, we shouldn't let 'perfect' by the enemy of 'good' – programmes take time to evolve and grow, so it's best to accept imperfections and make the most of what is working.

Deciphering inductive-deductive, qual-quant, and other research jargon that determines your success

According to Watson, Sherlock Holmes achieves most of his success through his powers of deduction. That's only one way of getting answers, though. The main two approaches to research are inductive and deductive. You'll also hear 'quant' and 'qual' data collection techniques bandied about. Feel free to look up the academic definitions and wade through what the professors have to say, but what follows is a commercial researcher's take on it, based on running research in practice – not in theory.

An inductive research approach starts with a blank sheet of paper and assumes nothing. You don't have a hypothesis to try and prove or disprove. There isn't a body of data to start with; no assumptions or preconceptions. You'll start with an objective or question, then explore what you find until it starts to take shape.

There are scenarios where firms unknowingly start with this approach, and it's usually when someone decides, 'Hey, we need a client listening programme'. Why? 'Well, everyone else seems to have one, and so should we.' There's not a business problem to diagnose; you're just going to start researching and see what you find. At some point you'll probably switch to deductive reasoning – but not at the outset.

By contrast, a deductive research approach is employed when you *already know* some things about the area you want to investigate, and you're going to attempt to prove or disprove ideas you already hold. You might start with a problem you want to solve: client-churn is high versus industry average – so why is that, and how can we reduce it? You might have an inkling, a theory about what the problem is: our client portal is a nightmare and it's ruining our client onboarding experience.

This is a simplification of the terms but it is worth thinking about when you're setting up a feedback mechanism in the first place – it's a form of research, and what's the basis for it? There are different scenarios whereby one approach is more suitable than the other; it's common to cycle between them, having an exploratory inductive phase and a more dogmatic deductive phase.

This comes to being in choosing data collection tools. In most B2B professional services cases, it's a choice between conducting personal interviews and running online surveys. There are, of course, other means, which we'll come back to later in this chapter. However, 90 per cent of the time the choice is between these two.

Generally speaking, personal interviews are far superior to online surveys for an inductive approach. It's a conversation in which you can pursue any line of thought that occurs to interviewer or interviewee; the constraints are few. Open-ended questions are appropriate and will garner extensive descriptions, with rich explanations and rationalisations. By contrast, it's rare that respondents to online surveys provide more than the minimum response to questions. People will happily tick boxes, reorder items, and give rating scores, but getting them to type more than a sentence or two is a challenge. Generally, they need to be very upset about something or feeling effusive about an experience, to want to describe it.

You can see from this comparison that interviews are best for inductive approaches where you want meaningful discussion, in order to understand issues and what the options might be. Meanwhile, surveys are better suited for deductive research where you've already established what the options can and should be, and you want people to choose between them so you can quantify the overall sentiment or preferences of a larger number of people.

This is why it usually makes sense to start with personal interviews before online surveys. One is not overall better than the other; they should be viewed as tools with different advantages and disadvantages, best deployed depending on your needs and objectives. Both have their place.

Moreover, a rounded client feedback programme cannot be static, freighted with the assumption that everything of importance is being covered with one set of permanent questions. That sort of complacency eventually leads to an irrelevant exercise, with declining participation rates and receding relevance to the business. Over time, it makes sense to use methods that generate new insights but be prepared to drop questions once no new learnings emerge and instead test new ones.

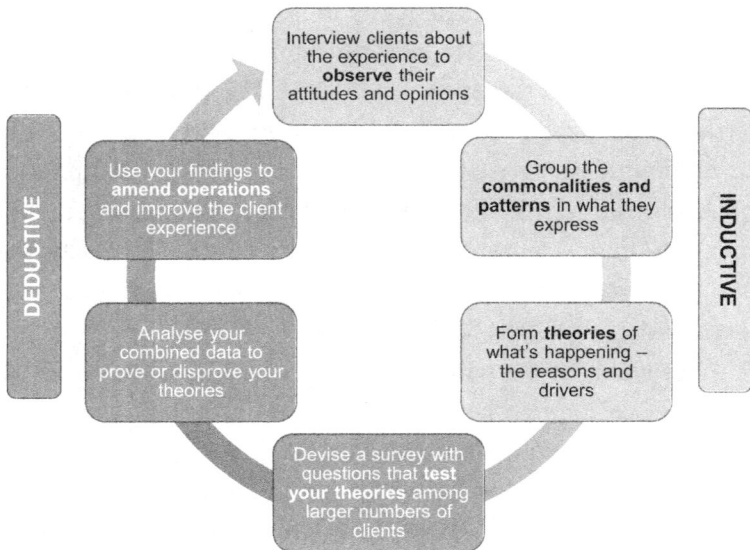

The best firms realise this and make use of both interviewing and surveying. It gives them an advantage because people respond to stories as well as to statistics. A report full of hard data and statistics might be packed with evidence but oftentimes makes no sense until it's accompanied by an anecdote told in a colourful way. Your office's meeting rooms might get poor scores within the facilities section of a survey, and so what? Only when a client talks about spending hours in there during a deal and compares the drab grey surroundings to a prison cell serving up stewed tea and stale biscuits does it drive home that it would be worth giving the room a lick of paint and upgrading the catering. These are very small things for clients worth huge sums, but easily get overlooked without a narrative underpinning the scores.

It's in this context of numbers versus words that you hear researchers referring to qualitative and quantitative research data. As with deductive and inductive research approaches, you can find very accurate discussion and definition of these terms in academic literature. Equating quant with numbers or with online surveys and qual with words or personal interviews is just outright wrong. Inaccurate. Misleading. Oversimplifying. But you know what? It is useful as a shortcut. It's like hearing someone misuse or mix up a term, but does it matter if you know what it is they're trying to say and it's helped convey their intention to you?

In general, you'll hear what comes out of interviews, what comes from an inductive approach, from open-ended, wordy or conceptual discussion as resulting in qualitative data. It's not necessarily so but handy as a reference point. Meanwhile, surveying that has numeric, countable, quantified outputs gets put in the quantitative data pile. The distinction is not correct because there is plenty of cross-over in approaches, techniques and methods. Often you can take descriptive data, code it and quantify it in order to understand it. Ratings and scores can, and usually do, need to be described to be understood. Quantitative data often has the appearance of being very objective – it's concrete and unquestionable. However, the way it is arrived at depends on subjective factors – the wording of questions, the means and context of collecting those responses.

The point is to be aware of the terms, understand how they get used and misused, and to moreover think about your purposes and the extent to which you want each element to serve your overall objectives. When you stand up in front of a room of executives to summarise your research, is it going to be sufficiently convincing to have tables of data or bar charts? Or do you want a series of stories to tell that come first-hand from a recognisable individual? The best communicators use both logos and pathos to create persuasive messages that appeal to both the rational and emotional sides of the human psyche.

You can prepare yourself for objections by anticipating this issue: 'You're telling us that you think we should change our investment strategy based on… half a dozen anecdotes / purely on these numbers?' If you've gone solidly down one route and excluded the other, you may regret it when you're asked either for empirical evidence or else some plausible real-world examples.

Other potential methods of gathering feedback, not all necessarily recommended

Besides personal interviews and online surveys, there are other ways of gathering client feedback. That is, other forms of primary research whereby you actively go out to collect it, as well as secondary research, whereby the data has already been gathered (perhaps for some other purpose) and is available to you.

Of that more active approach, the focus group is the most common. This is where you get a number of people together in a room, virtually or physically, ply them with food and drink, then give them a series of topics to discuss. You might segment your audience so that you have people of a similar demographic together, or else deliberately mix them up. With the former, it's then easier to compare and contrast different groups of individuals. A room of finance directors will tend to focus on different subjects than do a group of owner-managers. With the latter (a diverse array of individuals), you get to play off individuals against each other. Not in an antagonistic sense, more for provocation purposes: you want interaction among people, sparking discussion and debate. The idea is that the discussion will be more detailed and wide-ranging than would result from a one-to-one interaction with a researcher.

Advertisers seem to love this sort of approach. Perhaps because it's fun to be a fly on the wall. They're often used to uncover emotions related to selection and purchasing. You can explore subjects in an unstructured way. It's great for discussing potential new products and services – understanding how people imagine they might use them, how they'd go about choosing, and what would suit them best.

There are clear drawbacks, from a B2B perspective, of using focus groups when you are interested in focusing on an individual, where that person is a single point of dependency for your firm's revenue. You want their singular opinion on your services and interspersing their experience with that of others is unhelpful. The ability to express opinion is often limited by the fact that there are restrictions of commercial confidentiality.

The best possible application is where you have a number of colleagues from the same client organisation coming together to discuss your services. You won't get as much from each individual and there are problems relating to group dynamics that affect candour. However, there can be a pay-off in creating a fun relationship-building experience that in itself reflects well on the firm for offering a collaboration and listening opportunity.

Bear in mind that you need a competent focus group facilitator. The job is different from an interviewer conducting one-to-one interviews. The facilitator not only poses questions or raises topics for discussion: they need to manage the group. For example, they must know how to handle an individual with strong opinions to counter their dominance over the conversation, bring in those less vociferous, and ensure that everyone has an opportunity to express their opinion. You need this to avoid pre-emptive consensus whereby people don't want to contradict what seems to be the opinion of others (it may just be one person banging on about something but everyone assumes that's the prevailing view of the rest of the group, since nobody else is objecting).

If you have a group of strangers, rather than a number of colleagues, then the facilitator also has the task of breaking the ice between participants to ensure smooth interaction once you move into the main topics of discussion.

Due to the number of people involved and the accompanying logistics, followed by the time-consuming task of unpicking the conversations and contributions of individuals, focus groups are not a cheap or quick solution. Simultaneously, an hour with six individuals in a focus group does not generate as much insight as six one-hour interviews with individuals.

Secondary research sources, where the feedback has come via another means, include comments and ratings from social media posts, public review sites and directories, as well as more formal client complaints made by way of official apparatus. These can be valuable sources but the fact that you haven't actively set out to gather that feedback means it will likely come with an agenda, one that may or may not complement your purposes.

Public review sites and directories tend to contain feedback from highly loyal or especially delighted clients who, in many cases, have been prompted or in some way incentivised to give feedback. The effect is to boost the firm's profile and position in search rankings. At the other end of the spectrum, these sites register feedback from those who are severely irked by a dramatic service failure, who are out for vengeance and aim to inflict as much damage on the firm's reputation as possible.

In both scenarios, you've little or no control over the sample selection and there is inbuilt bias in what you get. It has its uses, but it can't be treated in the same way as a feedback study you commission, design, and undertake yourself. You've not decided the questions and the focus. Nor is it necessarily feedback from the clients you are most interested in.

Finally, there's also informal feedback: comments made directly or indirectly and picked up in conversation. You might call it gossip; you might call it feedback. This depends, perhaps, on whether you believe it or not. While sometimes very useful, it's difficult to verify and incorporate into a feedback programme. Sometimes it gets recorded in CRM systems or in account folders, but much of it is too ad hoc and unstructured to get used.

All these secondary sources of feedback can be valuable, but none tend to be as rich and focused as the data you actively collect via the likes of interviews and surveys. Nonetheless, where possible, it makes sense to feed as many of these sources into your programme as possible to make it a comprehensive listening tool. It's the occasional unexpected feedback from sources you might have otherwise overlooked that can prompt you to adjust the sights of your main programme, although you need to be discerning and take less well-substantiated feedback with a pinch of salt.

Surveying everyone: decision-makers, influencers, and end-users

As well as *how* you ask, it equally matters *who* you ask. Even more so than in B2C, in B2B not all clients are equal. The Pareto principle (or the 80-20 rule if you prefer Richard Koch's interpretation) has been done to death, but it does hold true in respondent selection nonetheless. If you analyse client lifetime-value at most firms, you find frightening disparities regarding the firm's income sources. A few clients are much more important than any of the others. With no exaggeration, you'll find up to 80 per cent of revenues dependent on just 20 per cent of clients.

At some point, someone will show up to a meeting and start asking about whether the results of your client research will be statistically significant, and whether you'll be able to extrapolate the findings and apply them to the firm's entire client base. You'll need to tell that person they've pitched up to the wrong meeting. This is commercial – not academic – research: we follow the money. The people spending the most, matter more than the others. If you're getting started and want to immediately deliver an outsized benefit to the firm, then start by surveying those clients with the biggest current and potential spend.

The goal is not necessarily to perfect client experience across the board, whereby everyone is treated equally, as nice as that might be for everyone. It's to optimise it with a focus on those clients who are key to the economics of your firm.

If selecting the right organisations to have participate is obvious, then selecting the right individuals to participate in a feedback exercise is more of a quandary.

It's quite likely that at a key client organisation you'll have multiple points of contact. Some will be senior decision-makers who get involved at the purchase stage and again at key points in the journey, but often won't even be using your service or interacting with staff on a day-to-day basis. Meanwhile, those at the coalface, interfacing with your people and services daily may have little, if any, say over which providers are used. Or, as is often the case, there's a mixture of the two whereby people might occasionally use the service directly, and might be consulted at certain points in the buying cycle.

Lots of different terms get used when it comes to classifying these different individuals concerning their role in purchase decisions. They all tend to fall into one of three categories, which for simplicity we'll call decision-makers, influencers, and end-users.

It's worth understanding whom you are surveying and ensuring that you reach a number from each group. Otherwise, the risk is that you get a green light indicating everything is fine (four out of 16 points of contact responded with positive ratings) only to find out that while end-users were happy, the decision-makers never knew it. When it's vice-versa, you *might* get away with the poor service you've been delivering but it's only a matter of time before the message makes its way up the chain.

Many firms make the mistake of pandering to the opinions of the most senior points of contact in the client organisation. Asked who should be surveyed, many partners will proudly provide the contact details of the chief executive or another C-suite individual (usually with a reminder to the effect of how busy they are and how you shouldn't trouble them for more than thirty seconds of their time). They don't mention that there are half a dozen people they've interacted with in the last year, let alone the dozen more that members of their team have dealt with.

Now, this is a good thing because most of the time you *do* want that top-of-the-cake person's point of view. The trouble is, sometimes that person is only mildly involved in the corporate relationship. In some cases, they are, in fact, only an influencer – they appreciate all that free hospitality the relationship partner lavishes on them, but if their operations person told them they needed to sack you tomorrow, well, sorry to break it to you. It's over. Often, the feedback from the most senior person isn't the most enlightening because they are relying on lots of second-hand accounts as to how your firm is performing. The General Counsel at a large insurance company has an army of claims handlers dealing with your lawyers. They don't speak to them regularly; instead, they rely on middle managers reporting in occasionally.

What we want in feedback is to see perspectives at all levels in which there is interaction. That's even if we're going to discount some of those later on, at the analysis stage, for whatever reason. You want to start by knowing everything.

Select participants based on financial value, not representative sampling

B2B feedback programmes run into trouble when attempting to take an overly academic approach to research. You're not a university trying to further human knowledge, nor the Office for National Statistics, bound by various commitments to government.

Rather than seek a representative sample of clients to survey and generalise about, the ideal approach is to simply survey EVERYBODY – if they spent money with you, they are a client.

If they are a client, you should want to know what they like and dislike about your offering. Online surveying is dirt cheap, and can be done at scale.

The only reason not to survey is if you feel you don't have the capacity to address the volume and type of service issues that may be raised. (Don't ask unless you're going to act.) Otherwise, survey everyone. And if you do have constraints that mean you can't reach everyone in one hit, how do you decide which clients to focus on? The simplest criteria to apply is value: what are they currently worth in sales? Apply an 80-20 approach and start with high value key clients. You want as much bang for your buck as possible. It makes no commercial sense to wring your hands, wondering if every voice is being heard, if it means getting feedback from a client worth 0.01 per cent of your annual revenue and – in so doing – ignoring one worth 10 per cent. There are other spheres where diversity and representation are crucial, but in client retention money talks, and rightly so.

It leads on from this that your mode of research should also be driven by value. Personal interviewing, predominantly in the form of face-to-face web interview, is the natural choice for key clients, while you can more economically reach the longtail of clients using online surveys.

Element	Interview	Survey
Data	Best for qualitative insights – exploring experiences, motivations and preferences in depth	Best for quantitative insights – indicating scale and frequency of perceptions and preferences
Flexibility	Can be adapted on the fly and refined interview by interview	Limited amount of customisation and facility to refine questions
Sample	Time intensive to reach large numbers of participants but response rates are high	Easy to reach very large numbers of participants but response rates are low
Cost	Expensive and time-intensive to administer, best reserved for key clients	Cheap and quick to administer; suited to reaching the whole client base

Again, if you can't initially survey everyone, then simple criteria like *all clients who have been invoiced a sum over X amount in the last 12 months* is a straightforward way to begin. You can expand and refine your criteria later, but to begin with make it easy for everyone to understand. Of course, you may have exceptions – most often where you have only a sliver of work but it comes from a huge and highly desirable organisation. Naturally, you might make an exception due to that particular client's growth potential. Or, because you want to expand into a sector that doesn't currently reap much reward financially but would if you committed more resource.

Choose a headline metric (NPS, CSAT, CES) that everyone can get behind

You're going to be gathering a vast array of information across a variety of different touchpoints, via many different questions from a whole host of different client stakeholders. How do you avoid paralysis by analysis and be able to deliver a clear message back to the business? You need something simple yet meaningful, something that everyone 'gets'. You need a consistent reference point that is reliable and trackable over time. This is the thing that everyone will rally behind. In short: you need a headline metric.

The goal with a headline metric is that you could pitch up at anyone's desk in the business (be it the managing partner, receptionist, trainee), and they would know what the firm's main client experience metric is. More than that, they can describe how it works – how the feedback is collected, and what the latest score means for the firm. And most critical of all: they know how their work, on a day-to-day basis, directly contributes to that score.

This last bit is crucial: everyone in the business should feel accountable in their role to that measurement of client experience. When it's going up there's going to be a sense of pride, especially – for instance – if it's higher than a competitor's. When the score is down, they'll want to know why and whether it's connected to their work.

This is not a metric that only appears in executive reports. At some firms, the number will be in every internal newsletter; it might be there on the extranet homepage as the first thing you see when you log in; it might be displayed on monitors around the office and in the lobby. It will permeate the consciousness of the organisation. By being on display it says that client experience, client perception, client feedback is important.

There are three main contenders to consider as possible headline metrics, each with pros and cons. Which you select is less important than the fact you should have one and use it consistently throughout the firm, across all locations and departments.

CSAT – Customer Satisfaction

Customer satisfaction (or *client* satisfaction as we'll refer to it as a more professional services friendly term) is the most widely recognised headline metric. It can be used to gauge satisfaction with the service delivered by the firm overall, but with specific service lines too. It's an element in most client-facing surveys, and can be used as a key performance indicator to track changes over time and identify elements of service requiring attention.

You calculate CSAT scores through responses to questions in the vein of 'How satisfied are you with XYZ?' Such questions are usually on a numerical scale, with either five, seven or 10 points. A 10-point scale has more nuance to it, but a five-point scale is the most common, with 'very dissatisfied' signifying the '1', and 'very satisfied' attributed to the '5' at the other extreme of the continuum.

Where you want to base your CSAT off one question, here are some examples:

- How satisfied are you with the firm?
- How satisfied are you with the work of the firm over the past 12 months?
- How satisfied are you with the outcome of your most recent interaction with the firm?

To calculate your CSAT, take the number of satisfied customers (those who rated you '4' or '5'), and divide by the total number of responses. For example, if 62 of your 100 responses have a rating of four or five, your score would be 62.

To understand the driver of CSAT, you'll need to look at other service scores in your questionnaire or the client segments. For example, CSAT scores might be higher for new clients versus longstanding ones or vice-versa, informing you that there are issues.

You can get more out of CSAT by upgrading it to an index. Rather than only ask about satisfaction overall, you break down the main service elements and get ratings for those. You then apply a weighting to each, based on how important the element is.

Multiply the weighting factor by the CSAT score for each element to produce a weighted score. Then, convert the score out of 10 into a percentage. This gives you your index score.

The main advantage of CSAT is that because the questioning is simple it's a direct way of spotting strengths and weaknesses, and therefore knowing what needs improvement. You can track customer satisfaction by touch points or lifecycle stages to see where you're not meeting expectations.

Service element	CSAT	Weighting	Weighted Score
Responsiveness	8	20%	1.6
Understanding needs	9	18%	1.62
Communication	10	18%	1.8
Documentation quality	8	16%	1.28
Advice quality	7	14%	0.98
Professionalism	9	14%	1.26
Weighted average	**8.54**		

CES – Customer Effort Score

Most literature calls CES the Customer Effort Score but again, for our professional services purposes, it's the *Client* Effort Score. Rather than satisfaction as an outcome to rate, the focus is on the input from a client perspective: the effort put in to get something resolved or – more generally – the ease of the experience. Essentially, how easy is your firm to deal with?

The origin of CES is a Harvard Business Review article published in 2010 called 'Stop Trying to Delight Your Customers', which argued that exceeding expectations doesn't necessarily make clients more loyal. Instead, the premise is that less effort in interacting with you predicts higher likelihood of repeat custom.

There are a few different wording examples of the question itself, but it's always along the lines of 'How much effort did you have to put into...', or 'How easy or difficult was it to deal with the firm?' The original version used a five-point scale from 'very low' to 'very high' but it works equally well on a 10-point scale labelled 'a lot of effort' to 'no effort at all', with the added benefit of more granularity.

CES can be used in different ways within a feedback programme but tends to be most useful in post-transaction surveys that come very soon after an interaction. For instance, straight after a support call or after a purchase. It can be helpful when comparing and contrasting experience with your different departments. You might find your corporate team are easier to deal with than your tax team, or vice versa, for instance. It's best when attached to a specific touchpoint or place in the client journey. However, it can also be used to measure the overall experience with your firm.

CES is a good candidate as your headline metric when you're aiming to provide an 'effortless experience' which may be more suited to some service lines than others.

Benchmarks for CES are not widely available, meaning that tracking and comparison are usually dependent on your firm's own data collection. You'll be comparing performance across your own departments, teams, and locations rather than against competitors or industry standards.

CES isn't as directly about loyalty or retention as other key metrics, but it is good for diagnosing issues that impact client experience. Combined with verbatim comments, CES is highly specific and actionable, meaning that you can identify the obstacles to a positive client experience and work on rectifying them. Being easy to deal with lends itself to use in marketing literature as a selling point, much more so than claims that 'most of our clients are loyal' – so what?!

NPS – Net Promoter Score

You want clients to use you again and again because it's cheaper than going out to win new ones. And you want them to tell other people because word of mouth is cheaper than other types of advertising. These are the principles underpinning Net Promoter Score (NPS): loyalty and recommendations.

NPS originated in Bain & Company under Fred Reichheld. It's deceptively simple, looks like CSAT, but works differently. Clients are asked a variant of the question: 'How likely are you to recommend the firm to a friend or colleague?' and respond on a scale of zero to 10. Sometimes it will be 'friend or family member' but 'peer or colleague' is more appropriate for B2B interactions. Based on the rating, clients fall into one of three categories: nines and 10s are 'promoters', sevens and eights are 'passives' and sixes and below are 'detractors'.

At an individual level, promoters are regarded as those clients most likely to be advocates of the firm, likely to repurchase often, cost relatively little to service (they've fewer complaints), and are most likely to spread positive word of mouth to others through referrals.

Meanwhile, passives may be sufficiently satisfied with the service they receive but they are not ardently loyal to the firm. They're not invested enough to bother complaining when service is below par. They are not likely to be actively seeking to defect to a competitor; however, the low affinity they feel means they are often more cost-sensitive and vulnerable to approaches from others.

Finally, detractors are explicitly unhappy in their relationship with your firm. They are likely to be publicly spreading negative word of mouth and actively seeking to defect to an alternative provider.

These individual ratings and categories are not an end in themselves. To calculate your firm's Net Promoter Score, you subtract the percentage of detractors from the percentage of promoters (ignoring the percentage of passives). The score is represented as a single number falling anywhere between -100 and +100. For example, if 10 per cent of clients are detractors, 40 per cent passives and 50 per cent promoters, then your NPS calculation would be 50 minus 10, giving you an NPS of 40.

A positive NPS tells you that more clients are acting positively than negatively in relation to your firm. What constitutes a 'good' NPS depends on your industry, as scores vary greatly depending on the business you're in. Fortunately, it's such a commonly used metric that it's relatively easy to find points of comparison to other firms and against other industries.

The fact that you can compare against B2C organisations is also an advantage in that it helps you to capture attention across the business by showing your NPS against, say, Apple, Tesla or whomever else might currently be an admired or maligned brand.

NPS is best used to measure sentiment toward the firm as a whole. However, it can work whereby you take scores by practice or department too, in order to pinpoint strengths and weaknesses in delivery. To get the most out of the question, it should be paired with an open-ended prompt along the lines of 'What's the main reason for that score?', which provides facility to praise or criticise, helping you to better understand the loyalty drivers.

Choosing between CSAT vs CES vs NPS

What is it we want to get out of a headline metric? It should be easy to get a score from your respondents. There should be benchmark data available you can compare performance against: your competitors, your industry, and other industries, for even more context. You should be able to set targets for improvement using the score so you know where you are now and where you want to get to in future. Beyond the 'one number', you want to be able to break down your headline metric by segment – it should make sense at individual and at aggregated level. Finally, it should tie in with service performance or client experience measures to enable you to perform driver analysis – to understand which elements contribute to that overall headline score.

Based on these criteria, all three metrics stand up as good candidates to headline. CSAT is no-nonsense, easily understood, works on an index basis, can be applied to touchpoints and transactions so is good for driver analysis, and is widely used by others so has available benchmarks. CES is user-friendly, highly specific and therefore actionable, has proven links to loyalty prediction but falls down on the benchmarking front, being a less popular metric than the others.

NPS is less intuitive than the others, as a construct and how the figure is calculated. However, its widespread popularity in both B2B and B2C makes it the best for benchmarking purposes, as well as being effective in driver analysis. The fact that its promoter, passive, detractor categories have become common currency in client experience tracking makes it a compelling option.

If it's not already clear, in most cases NPS is the best option as your headline benchmark to use across all your surveying, to incorporate into executive-level reporting, and behind which to rally your workforce. It's by no means perfect – you can find criticism of its statistical flaws in reputable journals. But no metric is perfect.

Nor does using it as your headline rule out using other metrics alongside it. Much of the best client research uses a combination. For example: CSAT for client experience touch-points; CES to gauge with which departments clients experience the most friction; and then NPS to understand resulting loyalty toward the firm. For once, you *can* have your cake and eat it. Just ensure the focus is attached to only one of these.

Start with relationship surveying before post-transaction

The feedback you receive, regardless of your choice of metrics, will vary depending on when you ask and whether you want a response to a specific interaction or an overall sum of all inter-actions. The terms commonly used to describe this are 'relation-ship' and 'transaction' surveying.

Relationship surveying is used when we want to capture overall sentiment or performance ratings. In B2B this is com-monly asked once a year, but the exact frequency matters less than consistency, which enables you to monitor trends and act where you see any dips. The questioning may cover many dif-ferent elements of the corporate relationship, various different types of interactions that may have taken place, and will explore some of the less specific, accumulated aspects of experience.

By contrast, measuring a specific event relating to a direct client interaction, the term is usually 'transaction' or 'post-trans-action'. The timing is dictated by the event, aiming to be as im-mediate as possible afterwards, while the memory is fresh. There will be fewer questions in total and they will be centred on the interaction that has taken place, tending to focus on par-ticular touchpoints or 'moments of truth'.

A good feedback programme will deploy both relationship and transaction surveying. The relationship survey is the back-bone of the programme, which is conducted on a consistent and regular basis. Transactional surveys are a more flexible tool employed at certain times and in particular instances. There are two common scenarios. The first relates to large or unusual matters that are strategic or transformational for the client. Advice and support given around an M&A deal, for instance, where the firm may have worked with the client very closely and intensely and the outcome will have had a significant impact on the organisation.

The second use case for transactional surveying is to investigate a particular stage or set of touchpoints in the client journey. You might introduce the surveying temporarily to work out what's going on, and determine what an appropriate remedy might be. For instance, one department or practice frequently introduces another but that other department fails to sell its services. Is the handover being done poorly or is the second practice inept in some way? A survey that is triggered after that introduction to test the handover or onboarding with that other practice records the client experience at that point – you monitor the outcome later on (for example, the subsequent spend with that practice) and then try to derive the key success or failure factors involved at that touchpoint.

Transactional surveying gets to the nub of distinct issues, while relationship surveying is a barometer for overall sentiment and for exploring client experience more broadly.

Type	Frequency & Touchpoints	Operational Use	Strategic Use
Relationship Feedback	Set intervals from onboarding onwards to annual in-depth reviews and off-boarding	- Relationship management - Pipeline analysis - Sales and account management performance	- Competitive analysis - Brand messaging - Client segmentation - Investment decisions
Transaction Feedback	On-demand (client defined) or post-matter (triggered by value), post-pitch debriefs	- Account recovery / growth - Account team coaching - Performance management	- Quality improvements - Process improvements - Resource investments

A common question you face when devising a new feedback programme is whether to start with transactional or relationship surveying, or employ both simultaneously. Do this: start with relationship surveying. You get overall perception and from that you will come up with hypotheses of what needs more detailed examination. It's a gentler start to the feedback journey – add the transactional surveying later when there is less resistance internally and you've won the confidence of clients having shown them the firm will actually act on feedback and therefore it's worth their time doing detailed reviews of specific events. It's likely that, to start with, you don't have the resource or infrastructure to deal with transactions (getting the right trigger information from practice management systems, for instance); you do know that the client exists from the billings, even if you don't know the timings or nature of the work.

Takeaways

- Choose between personal interviewing and online surveys but where possible, use a combination of the two methods, collecting both rich stories and detailed stats – you want both to persuade and activate.

- Only if you want interaction between respondents are focus groups helpful, for example, if you want to generate new ideas. Otherwise, interview separately as you'll get more insights from each individual.

- Other sources of feedback such as complaints, public review sites, and social media posts can all be useful too but keep in mind that they are generated for specific reasons and come with their own biases.

- When it comes to sampling, follow the money. Rather than worry about representative sampling, make sure you have feedback from the clients that account for the majority of spend with the firm.

- Always start with relationship feedback and only then try to implement transactional feedback: the latter invariably runs into problems with identifying matters and extracting data from CRM systems.

CHAPTER 5
HOW TO CONDUCT IN-DEPTH PERSONAL INTERVIEWS

Get closer than ever to your customers. So close, in fact, that you tell them what they need well before they realise it themselves.

—Steve Jobs

These people's time is at an enormous premium – we want to extract every last drop of value from each and every second of interaction. We want insights that every part of the firm can use to maximise the relationship and use at scale with other clients. And yet, an interview is itself part of the client experience, hence it needs to be a positive and stimulating experience that justifies the interviewee's time investment. It's a big challenge, but an achievable one.

The relationship partner isn't the best person to conduct a feedback interview

If there was a first rule of interviewing, it would be this: you should never have the relationship partner or primary point of contact for the relationship conduct the feedback interview. Ideally, nobody who is involved in the day-to-day at all. There are plenty of alternative options, along with reasons why they'll do a better job.

It's probably obvious to you already, but the person leading service delivery can't be objective about the relationship. You need detachment from the intricacies of the relationship. The last thing you want is for the interviewer to get bogged down in the technical elements of service delivery – we're there to talk about the experience, not to get defensive when criticised or else try to sell additional services because the client is clearly very happy.

Nonetheless, you will face opposition to having someone else involved. It's natural, especially where either there is something to hide (they know the client has some gripes and would rather they not be aired) or the relationship is sailing along very profitably, so why risk some outsider messing things up? These are reasonable points. This is why you need an interviewer who is competent; someone you can trust.

The solution some firms use is to introduce a member of the firm who is not involved in the account, who offers a degree of independence and is credible. They are given a title for the purpose, along the lines of Independent Advisory Partner. They come from a different practice area or department and aren't known to the client. They're often approaching retirement or already semi-retired, and are cutting back on their own client-facing work.

Other firms will train up a business development specialist for the job. Either route can work to some extent because you are creating a degree of independence. These options are okay, and better than nothing. Just whatever you do, don't have your senior or managing partner or other C-suite exec undertake it. It will kill your programme. Firms draft in top management because they think it shows key clients how valued they are, and at the same time helps leadership stay close to the burning issues. There is some logic there but it means a long slow death. Their time is at a premium, so it takes months to get interviews scheduled; they are terrible at recording the interview accurately, or else depend on a PA attending; and – even if it's not their client – ultimately, they are responsible for that client's experience, so are not independent. You can't expect them to remain detached. At the same time, the client doesn't want to bring up minor nitty-gritty issues with that most senior person – they will feel that they are trivialising the exercise to bring up anything but 'strategic' matters, and so pain points get missed.

Whether it is the managing partner, a so-called independent partner, or anyone else from within the business, the client can't have a genuinely candid conversation with the assurance that everything won't be reported back. There is no intermediary buffer. This will be no surprise to you, but you should use someone genuinely independent if you want unadulterated feedback that is designed to help you improve. Clients recognise these issues and see through PR exercises.

This is not to say that top management shouldn't be involved. Indeed, they come into their own and should get in front of clients at the later remediation stage rather than in the discovery phase of feedback.

Besides these relationship reasons, there are also practical considerations. A good research interviewer has a set of characteristics and skills that are learned and developed over time. They come from conducting interviews day in, day out. They know how to tease out pain-points and explore opportunities. If you want to become one of these rare creatures, or else hire one to be your research partner, the following advice is for you.

Avoid interviewing more than one person at a time

What if you've identified more than one person from the same client organisation who is worth allocating the time and money to interview? How many participants are optimal on a single call? It's simple: if you can, don't interview more than one person at a time. An interview is meant to be a one-to-one conversation. If you involve more than one interviewee, then it's a focus group. Focus groups are useful, but serve different purposes: debating topics, bouncing ideas around, getting people to share their experiences in an open forum.

You should avoid having multiple interviewees primarily because one person will dominate within a group. Usually, the more senior person gets the first say in answering questions and the more junior person tends to toe the line. You can see it in interview transcripts by looking at the order of answers and word count per participant. That's even when the boss has the self-awareness to let others speak. If you want the opinion of more than one person, then ask them to give their views independently – otherwise their view will be diluted.

At a practical level, having multiple interviewees is simply harder to record accurately. You get significantly more crosstalk, where people speak over each other or interrupt. They're also more difficult to schedule, given that senior people have busy diaries. The interview itself will take more time also. A 40-

minute interview will become a 60-minute interview with two people, a 90-minute interview with three – it takes more time for everyone to voice their views and there will be more discussion. Again, you might want this if the aim is to explore new ideas in some way, in which case you should run a focus group instead.

Interviewees will sometimes think they are helping the interviewer by offering to interview together, not appreciating that it will actually cost them more time, individually and collectively. To avoid this, don't email the target interviewees together. Instead, contact them individually, albeit mentioning that other colleagues have also been asked to participate.

What if, nonetheless, you do end up with two or three interviewees on a single call? The practicalities of interview management become important. Get everyone to introduce themselves so you are clear who everyone is – this is especially important on audio-only calls. Then, annotate each speaker's comments so you are clear as to whom is speaking, so there's no confusion later about who said what. Where you get an answer to your questioning from one individual only, try prompting the others to see if opinion varies. Likewise, offer the option to score separately to capture variation in opinion (by individual or department), rather than a blended score that misses divergent views.

Get a briefing in advance of the interview

If you're interviewing a senior executive at a key client then you should get a one-to-one briefing with the appropriate person at the firm. That's usually the relationship partner or account manager. Unless there's anything out of the ordinary to discuss, ten minutes on the phone should suffice.

For less critical client relationships, you might receive the information via a form. However, a personal briefing has the advantage of allowing you to discuss informal details that may not otherwise get committed to paper. These might be confidential matters, or simply the interviewee's personal quirks and pet peeves (that you should be aware of in advance). 'He's lovely but he's weird, so don't be surprised if he brings up X, Y or Z – this is the kind of comment you may encounter. It's also a more efficient use of everyone's time to have a quick conversation as opposed to endlessly chasing down written briefing notes.

In either format, it's essentially the same information you're looking for in preparation. It's a mini SWOT analysis of the commercial and interpersonal relationship.

You want to know the basics to begin with. What was the origin of the relationship? A longstanding personal friendship with one of the partners, or a hard-fought competitive tender that's up for renewal in six months? What range of services does the firm undertake for this client?

You should explore the proportion of work the firm currently receives overall and by practice or service line. Are the competitors already known? If so, which ones do which types of work? Beyond knowing the allocations of work, is spend with the firm increasing, decreasing or staying steady? Is the reason for that known?

If it's not obvious, what does this organisation do? If it's a large corporate you should have looked it up, but if it's a private business with only a one-page website then it's only reasonable to get an explanation now.

You want to know if there have been any big successes with the client and – more importantly – have there been any difficulties encountered? This can be difficult to admit to but it's crucial that you know where things have gone wrong. You're not going to raise the issue of a service failure, but if the interviewee mentions it you need to be able to nod sagely in acknowledgement (how could the firm possibly have sent you to discuss service if you didn't know about that million-pound shambles?!).

Having captured all the commercial background, you want to learn a little bit about your interviewee's role and responsibilities. It makes a difference whether they have a large team reporting into them or not, if they have a particularly stressful project coming to a close, or if they are just back from maternity leave. There are lots of little clues that will help you in understanding the individual and tailoring the way you pitch your questions. If you ask, 'What are they like as a person?' you'll find out whether you're about to go head-to-head with a detail-oriented number-cruncher or a laid-back blue-sky thinker. It helps to know in advance.

Finally, you should check if there are any additional questions to pose that aren't already covered in the questionnaire or a subject to focus on. You'll either be asked to pose a question that's already in the questionnaire (happens about half the time), something very specific about a recent piece of work (can be great for operational insights) or, quite often, to get competitor intelligence about what other firms are doing, which, while already baked in to most questionnaires is a nice challenge to have when you know what you gather will be especially valued.

One other consideration is what to do if you don't get a briefing prior to the interview. There are times when you can't get hold of anyone to give a briefing, either through lack of availability or downright disinterest. Clearly the latter is disappointing, but fortunately rare. The former should only be the case in exceptional instances also. Without a personal briefing, you'll still be fine, but it does mean you need to be especially diligent and attentive to compensate for your lack of inside line. Some people like going in cold without having been prejudiced by the firm's perspective on a relationship, but on the whole you get much more out of an interview with the extra preparation.

For better insights, don't make audio recordings of your interviews

How many times have you had a customer service call start with someone telling you that your call will be recorded for training and quality purposes? So, your instinct is that your client feedback interviews should be recorded too. You don't want to miss any little detail of what's discussed and you want to have the evidence later to back up any assertions you want to make. The reality is counterintuitive.

When someone is being recorded talking about their internet provider, gas supplier, or whatever 'small-time' service provider that only amounts to a few hundred quid per year, what does it matter what they have to say? There is no important relationship at stake. Switching is easy. If they have a gripe, they can get it off their chest. Meanwhile, call centres want to be able to take comments, aggregate, and track them at volume.

With high value B2B service feedback, our priority is to protect and nurture client relationships. To that end, there are two reasons why recording interviews runs counter to that purpose. One is psychological and the other practical.

First, you want your interviewee completely at ease. People behave differently when they know they are under observation. There are plenty of psychology experiments that show how people effectively put on a performance when they think that their words and actions may be scrutinised. A feedback interview should feel like a discreet conversation between two people. If what they say could potentially be played back to a room full of executives or via some other media online, they are going to be more guarded. Even those who explicitly tell you otherwise. You want the interviewee to be as completely frank and candid as possible, not worrying about the plausible deniability of any statement they've just made.

That's why taking a written (that is, typed) record of your meeting is superior. If ever that record does get referred to, the interviewee can say to the client partner or whomever, 'Ah, I think the interviewer misunderstood me there, or they didn't get it down right'. They have some 'wiggle room', which protects them and the relationship. Being able to save face matters more than the rare occurrence that something isn't perfectly verbatim.

In practical terms, try taking a look at what a truly verbatim transcript looks like. It's a baffling forest of false starts, *um's* and *ah's*, digressions about the weather, and a whole host of irrelevant content. People inadvertently talk over each other, stop to apologise, break off to answer calls from colleagues or take deliveries. A full transcript is long and convoluted and rarely will anyone thank you for making them wade through it.

Whether you use an automated recording system like the ones built into Microsoft Teams or you engage a professional transcriptionist, not only do you add delay to processing the output, you also add issues around confidentiality and data protection. At the end of the day, to have something valuable to share and present within your firm, you'll need to edit it anyway.

This is where a well-trained, experienced interviewer comes in. Not only can they hold an informed conversation – listening, responding, and posing relevant questions to keep the flow going – they can also accurately type out the conversation.

A good interviewer will capture about 80-90 per cent of what the interviewee says while simultaneously editing out irrelevancies in real time. At the end of the interview, they will spend time correcting their typos and filling out the various common abbreviations they'll have used but they'll have a transcript ready in short order.

It won't have every last word – like the bit where they apologise for getting up to let the dog out – but it will have, verbatim, what they had to say about your nearest competitor having invited them to a hospitality event, the exact figure they are planning for next year's budget, and every other nugget of relevance to your commercial business relationship.

What else is there to know in advance?

Regardless of whether you've had a detailed briefing, some cursory notes on the back of envelope, or nothing at all, you should at least have a quick look for yourself. Save this for the 10 minutes or so you have before starting, while sipping your brew and getting into the right mindset. A recap is especially useful when it may have been weeks since the briefing.

Your best sources are the organisation's website where you can see if there have been any recent big announcements and look at the individual's profile. Usually, more revealing is their LinkedIn profile: it has more background, including education and interests. Finally, a Google search will sometimes bring up interesting press articles, depending on how high profile they are within their industry.

None of this amounts to any major sleuthing, but it is worth doing for the occasions when you're able to put two and two together in your subsequent conversation. They mention the need to get spiralling costs under control? You're able to drop in that, indeed, you've read about the problem with that new manufacturing plant. These are subtle cues that tell the interviewee that you are clued-up – their service provider has really invested in this feedback exercise by hiring someone on-the-ball and so it's worth taking seriously.

How to introduce yourself and begin the interview

Think about an interviewee's motivation for participating in a feedback interview. They are there to help the firm and because they think, or at least hope, taking part will aid the corporate relationship in some way. In part it shows they're willing to invest time but also that they might shape future delivery of services. Sometimes they have a specific agenda – there is an area for improvement they'd sorely like to see acted on and so they will give voice to that to push the firm to address it. Whatever the exact reason, they expect a positive and constructive interaction.

Besides a warm welcome and a touch of gratitude for them giving up their time, there are a few other things to cover in your introduction. You could prepare a script for yourself, but in order to have a natural interaction it's better to have a simple checklist of things to cover which you can mark off.

You should *thank* your interviewee for joining and assure them that you'll aim to make it a constructive use of their time. This is to show you recognise that they are important and to make them feel appreciated. Don't go over the top in reminding them of their time, though – this is a pleasant break from other work; we don't want them to feel anxious about falling behind on other things!

You should remind them that the *purpose* of the exercise is to gather feedback that the firm will use to improve service: in the first instance for their benefit, but also across the business in the form of best practices. It's important to explain this to avoid confusion with any other exercise; this is not a self-serving directory review asking for snippets of praise to be used publicly.

You should explain that you are *independent* of the relationship and the reason for this is to enable a candid conversation. Explain that they'll be given an option at the end of the interview with regard to how their comments will be treated. The idea is that they can speak freely and if, at the end, they decide something shouldn't be relayed back as spoken, they have the opportunity to reword or redact it as they wish – the interviewer acts as a buffer to some extent, and can help them craft their message to the firm. Mention too any credentials that justify why you are the one conducting the interview.

You should add that you will be using a *questionnaire* with a set number of questions and taking typed notes. Also mention that there will be scoring questions but that what we're really interested in is the rationale behind the numbers. This stops your interviewee jumping into an unstructured diatribe; instead, they'll know to follow your lead in terms of subject. They'll also understand that you are recording their words in written form. Moreover, they know that you want explanation, that scores are not the most important thing – it's their thinking and feelings that matter.

You should reiterate the agreed interview *duration*. This gives them an opportunity to tell you if there is a hard-stop or whether they're in no rush. Be aware that much of the time you'll be told how busy they are, and even asked if you can keep it short, only to find that once they've settled in and are enjoying the conversation they are happy to talk all day. Most people are used to dire tick-box exercises – when they realise you are really listening, they'll engage and take the opportunity to share.

It's important to make these points at the start to provide context. It demonstrates this is a safe space for discussion and it heads off the majority of questions they might have about the process, allowing more time for the actual interview. It should only take you a minute to cover all the points. You can proceed smoothly by saying something along the lines of: 'Unless you have any questions about the process, then we'll start by talking about [first subject on the questionnaire]'.

How to lead and pace interviews for the best results

Once you're underway, as interviewer it's your job to control and pace the interview. You want to ensure that all the topics are covered in sufficient depth without running out of time. Simultaneously, you want to allow time for the elements that matter most to your interviewee. If they have a lot of useful insight around inconsistency between the firm's practices and, meanwhile, didn't have any sight of project financials, then obviously you'll need to focus on service experience and skim over the value and budget aspects.

Pacing is mostly about being sensitive to what most concerns your interviewee, and exploring the most relevant issues from their perspective. However, do not allow an interviewee to get overly fixated on single issues: where you feel you've captured an aspect of criticism or praise sufficiently, you need to move on. Your tone should be friendly and professional. Give reassurance that you have grasped the point and that you will see that it is given due attention. Simply repeat back a paraphrasing of the main point, checking if you've got it right, then say you want to make sure you cover all aspects of their experience.

Somewhat less frequently, you'll have interviews wherein you fly through the topics fairly quickly and have time to spare. While we want to get as much out of the time as possible, don't feel you need to wring out every last minute of interview time. If you've got clear insights and recommendations, then wrap up and your interviewee will go away happy that you've been true to your word in valuing their time. If, however, you've got time left and feel like something is missing, go back to any questions where you feel you've missed something and double-check if there's anything more to say. You can say something along the lines of 'Looking over my notes, it feels like we only touched lightly on that matter of availability. What I've understood is [insert detail]. Is that correct or do you have anything to add?' You don't want to over-egg a minor point, but if capturing extra detail might help with operational improvements later, then it's worth making sure you capture all the facts.

Make being interviewed an engaging, stimulating and useful experience

An ideal interview should feel like a natural conversation that flows through interesting and relevant topics. Although you've stated at the outset that there's a questionnaire you'll be using (in order to show that there is structure and process), there's no need to make it evident that you're working through it at every step.

In general, you should pose questions in a consistent manner from interview to interview, and – if drafted right to begin with – they should sound relatively colloquial anyway, so that you feel comfortable asking them. Questions that are to be used for benchmarking (or other types of tracking and comparison) should be asked word for word but with others, it's okay to rephrase them so that they flow.

It's also fine, and often a good thing, to deviate from the order questions appear in the questionnaire. This contributes to the sense of the interview as conversation. If you start with some questions about service but your interviewee makes a compelling point about, say, fees, then either you can let them know that you've got questions coming up about fees or else just move to that section, returning to the generic service questions later.

This gives a more tailored experience, utilises time for what matters most, and feels more natural than effectively being told 'No, I don't want your opinion on that right now – wait until later!'

The ability to jump around within a set of questions rather than work through them sequentially depends on your knowing your questionnaire in advance so that you can navigate it confidently.

The exception, where you should not roam around the question set, is when information needs to be revealed by the interviewer to ascertain unprompted knowledge. For example, if you've got a question that asks which practice areas the interviewee is aware of, then obviously you can't skip to a question that involves rating the main practices (prompting for scores) until you've asked the unprompted one.

Another aspect of the interview as conversation is your role as interlocutor. If you literally only ask the questions in front of you, it'll be a dry and dull experience that is unlikely to lead anywhere interesting. You may as well be substituted for a chatbot. Making it conversational relies on just a couple of main ingredients.

The first of these ingredients is your reaction to the interviewee's answers. You should feel free to react naturally – let your tone show when you're surprised, intrigued, confused, and so on. The same goes for body language. Most of the time, when on camera, you're reading questions and intently typing, but your interviewee isn't – they're looking back into the camera and seeing how you respond physically. You should show emotion in your body language. Seeing you react is visually encouraging, helping the interviewee to expand and share freely. If you were a couple of friends talking and you were hearing an interesting story, what sort of things would you say?

'Wow, really! And then what happened? What were you thinking at the time? So that wasn't what you were expecting? I'd be delighted, what did you do next?'

You don't need to be over-enthusiastic and gushing over every detail but when things are interesting and potentially useful for the firm to know, give off the signals to positively reinforce that.

Second to your reactions, are your contributions. An executive interviewer has knowledge and experience that aids the discussion in two ways. Not only are you familiar with the jargon and current industry affairs, but you hold an opinion. At certain times, you should express your view on a subject partly to show you understand what they have to say but also as a provocation. Not in an argumentative sense but with the aim to stimulate discussion of a subject. You usually preface it with something positive like 'That's interesting you think that, because…' and go on to introduce an idea along with your source: '…I read in The Times that…' or 'I was talking to a surveyor who said… and the prediction was that…'

This sort of interaction makes the meeting interesting. The big warning that goes with this, though, is that you must not talk too much. You are there primarily to listen. What you say should not be idle chit-chat but serve the purpose of enhancing and maximising the interview outputs. At a rough estimate, your words should be no more than 20 per cent of what's said in the interview – no matter your knowledge of a subject, you're a supporting actor and the interviewee is the star of the show.

Regulating the amount you have to say also helps reduce the likelihood that you lead the 'witness'. Having taken a briefing and researched the interviewee in advance puts you at risk of being biased in how you conduct the interview. You need to avoid introducing your prejudices in how you interact. For example, in the briefing the relationship partner may be concerned about a particular issue – obsessed, even. They might have spent half the briefing telling you about how everything went wrong on a particular project, how it was delayed, how the outcome was a disaster and so on. You go in with that knowledge, which is useful in forewarning you, but shouldn't necessarily lead you to shaping the entire interview around it, anxiously expecting a tirade of criticism. There are times when the interviewee will dismiss it out of hand: 'Yeah, we were a bit disappointed with that last one – it didn't go our way, but one blip in five years isn't bad and the latest work is excellent'. Clearly, you won't then dwell on it and pick at the scab – you move on to what is most relevant.

The other thing to remember is not to 'go native'. This gets harder the more detailed a briefing is – being told what a nightmare this particular client has been, for instance – but also when your relationship to the firm is longstanding. The danger is that, rather than act as an impartial intermediary, you form an allegiance to the firm and feel the need to defend the firm or partner. Your job is never to put up a defence. Even when what the interviewee has to say is pretty patently unfair, the exercise at hand is to listen, empathise, and to really understand the interviewee's perception. For them, their perception is reality and educating them otherwise is at the discretion of the firm later on.

In conducting the interview, you are collecting nuggets of opinion and insights that you'll pass on to be sorted through. You want to pick up on everything that seems relevant and that might later be teased out further by someone well informed within the firm. This isn't the forum to resolve problems or propose new directions; it's for recognising, exploring and understanding – laying a foundation for the actions that will follow.

Only occasionally might it be worth putting onus on the interviewee by asking, 'What can the partner do to put things right?'

Don't try and force front-end rapport – let it build

A successful interview feels like a conversation, not an interrogation. There's a questionnaire as a point of reference that guides discussion and ensures key topics get covered, but it shouldn't feel like a rote exercise of question and answer.

This leads some people to think that you need to make an overt effort to build rapport at the outset. However, a forced or artificial attempt at the starting point isn't necessary, and will feel false. The best rapport building is simply being a professional and well-informed interviewer.

That means showing empathy by exploring their concerns, acknowledging what something means for them personally and emotionally, and asking about and reflecting back the person's feelings.

The people we are interviewing are busy professionals. They know the purpose of the interview and expect to get on with the task, so you don't need more than a couple of minutes of general chat at the beginning.

If, as the conversation progresses, it's apparent that there is no rush, then feel free to talk more generally but we don't know the time pressure at the start, and so don't want to waste valuable time, only to discover that there is a hard close coming up and we still have 10 questions left to cover.

Use probing questions to clarify and expand

Some interviewees have the gift of the gab; they ramble on, wax lyrical; they give you every little detail about everything. Others are direct and to the point, bordering on monosyllabic. Regardless of the volume of words, and no matter how fine-tuned your questionnaire, you don't necessarily get the answer you're looking for at first. Usually, that's not deliberate – most people are trying to be helpful and they just don't always understand what you're looking for. However, on some subjects, people will be deliberately evasive, especially around sensitive topics such as price, competitors, or an underperforming team member. For this reason, we use probing questions to supplement our formally scripted ones.

A probing question is simply a follow-up to a question, and aims to get more detail or clarity from the interviewee. It doesn't necessarily even have to be phrased as a question. Sometimes they are prepared in advance and you can anticipate questions that will require elucidation, but usually you formulate and ask them 'on the fly'.

Where you are looking for clarity, you might use a closed question. The simplest is where someone is unsure of a rating. If they've said, 'Either a six or a seven' then you might ask, 'If you had to score either a six or seven, which would it be?' Or, you might check that you caught something correctly, and so you paraphrase what you heard, for example: 'You wouldn't use them again for this type of work because of the delays you experienced, is that right?' Usually, you get not only confirmation but further information.

More often, you'll use probing questions to encourage someone to expand on a point. For this, open-ended questions work best, for example, 'What else do you have to say about that?' Or, 'What do you think the firm should do next?'

Where someone needs coaxing, it can help to explain why you are pursuing a particular line of enquiry. Telling someone, 'I'm asking because I know the firm is committed to improving that aspect of service and your examples could help them better diagnose the problem' gives them licence to explain, reassured that the information is useful and will be used. (If it's something they've complained about previously and not seen improvement, they will naturally be reluctant to repeat themselves without some sign of commitment to action.)

A key probing question is to ask for an example. This is, literally, 'That's an interesting point, what would be an example?' This takes a vague point about, say, documentation being poor, which could entail a hundred different possible improvements, to learning that it's specifically the format – the documents would be easier to use if supplied as PDFs. Examples stop you from making blind assumptions about what needs to be fixed.

Similarly, asking your interviewee to compare and contrast something can give you concrete points of reference. If you've established that there is a competitor for similar lines of work, then if you're told the quality of advice wasn't good, ask, 'How does that compare with the competitor?' Here, you find out how another firm delivers the same thing, along with the ways in which the product is superior or at least different.

Another technique for when you've received a less than adequate answer is to return to it later, rephrase it slightly, and repeat the question. This can be particularly effective in asking about competitors. If you've touched on competition early on and the interviewee has demurred on the subject, but later on they've warmed up and become more open, then return to it again. You will often find that if you've conducted the interview in a professional and competent way, you'll have earned the right to talk about subjects the interviewee wasn't initially keen to cover.

How people interpret questions can depend on their personality. Some people are highly rational and literal. They get bogged down in the practical details and so struggle to answer without all the possible information available. You can help them circumnavigate these constraints by making it hypothetical. For example, 'You're probably right – they don't have the resource to fix that problem at the moment; let's say you had a magic wand – what would the perfect experience be like instead of what happened?'

Stepping out of reality can help people think laterally. You'll sometimes get what seem like very silly answers but they reveal their feelings and true desires when practical constraints are removed.

The thing to always keep in mind when probing is that your tone should remain positive and constructive; your purpose should evidently be to aid understanding between firm and client. If your interviewee seems uncomfortable, you need to back off and reassure that it's not essential – you're asking because you are curious and thought it could be helpful to know.

If you've asked about a competitor and – reading between the lines – been politely told to leave off, then don't push your luck. Make light of it if you can, 'I had to ask!' and move on to other matters. Always remember that the interviewee should be going away from the conversation with the sense that it was a stimulating exercise and a constructive use of their time.

Be prepared to deal with technology problems and other interruptions

Things will go wrong. It's inevitable. There'll be problems no matter how much effort you put into arranging calls at a convenient time or providing reminders and all the required information upfront. The good thing is that you know this, and so can be prepared.

By contrast to telephone interviews, video conference interviews suffer far fewer 'no shows' where the interviewee isn't available at the given time. The etiquette is different: it feels more like a properly organised meeting, and so most business executives will rarely leave you hanging. And when they do, it's usually because they're having a problem with the technology.

In anticipation, you should have some draft email copy at the ready to ping over to them. It should read along the lines of: 'Hi John, I'm in the Teams meeting room for our client feedback review. The link is <u>here</u>. If you're having any difficulty joining, please let me know and we can switch to good old-fashioned telephone if that helps.' Give it another five minutes and then call them by phone if you haven't had a response.

Yes, they are a big and important client but it's also reasonable that they be considerate and respect your time too. The majority of the time they're either having trouble because of something system-related at their end, or else a meeting has overrun and they didn't have your details to hand to let you know. Your email gives them opportunity to respond with a quick note.

If they turn up a couple of minutes late, it's no problem. If they join the meeting, say, 15 minutes late, then you may have an issue. If it's a 30-minute interview and you've only half the time normally allocated, then you need to ascertain if they have an extra 15 to tack on. If they don't, then postpone. Since you've got them there and then, find a time in your calendars and reschedule. There's just no way you can do justice to the exercise in a rush with half the intended time.

The same goes for interruptions. Your interviewee is head of HR and gets a call from the union about an impending strike.

Acknowledge that this is no longer a convenient time for them, and agree to pick up on 'Part Two' of your conversation later. We don't want rushed or distracted interviewees – the good stuff, in terms of insights, comes from people who are fully focused and present.

How to handle an interview that isn't going to plan

For the majority of the time, the feedback you receive is overwhelmingly positive. Most people are being interviewed because they are key clients, are prized by the firm, and are receiving the best service the firm has managed to devise to date. You'll be capturing best practice, unravelling a few niggles, and delving into possible areas for growth.

Then, on the odd occasion, there'll be a bombshell. The briefing will have told you this key client that's been with the firm for 10 years and represents 10 per cent of annual revenue is completely satisfied, totally safe and that the interview is probably unnecessary. You start interviewing and something just doesn't feel right.

Your interviewee gives short, polite, yet slightly curt answers. Looks a bit uncomfortable in their seat, glances at their watch, just isn't engaged. The scores might not be devastatingly bad. They might say relatively nice things about the partner.

This is when you should trust your instincts. Put the questionnaire to one side. Stop typing for a minute. The number one thing is to acknowledge here is that something's just not right. Perhaps something is not said. You can reference how the questionnaire is very standardised but actually it's not getting to the underlying issue here, is it? Ask, what is it we should really be talking about?

You are giving the interviewee an opportunity to step out of their role, in the same way you are stepping out of yours, to get to the real problem.

It's at this point you'll find out that, actually, the account is not going to be the firm's for much longer if service continues the way it is. It could be that the relationship partner has dropped the ball in some way. Either they've made a howler that they haven't owned up to, or else don't know about. The interviewee may not want to discuss it because they feel resentment; they may not feel they owe it to them to offer the opportunity to fix it.

Otherwise, it could be that the interviewee has no problem with the partner or firm, but that someone else – someone more influential in the hierarchy – has taken umbrage. It can also be that a corporate action of some sort means the future is bleak for some reason. Maybe it's something else entirely.

Whatever the source, the interviewer's job is to acknowledge that there's an issue, put the interviewee at ease, and try to tease out details of the issue before getting the interviewee to pose possible solutions. It won't be a quick fix but there are some first steps to at least get the firm or partner to understand what the problem is. You just want a stay of execution to buy time; your role is not to fix the problem, just to gather as much information about it as possible and be able to pass that on internally.

This is where it is especially important not to try to defend the firm, but explore the issue together, showing plenty of empathy – it must be difficult, frustrating, etc for that person – and formulating some next steps.

It's absolutely fine to abandon the questionnaire completely in favour of this. Nobody will care about whether the questions on added value were completed when the firm is potentially getting binned.

Similarly, following an interview of this nature don't necessarily follow the usual procedures in writing up: pick up the phone to the most appropriate person, in order to expedite and escalate the matter as quickly as possible. If ever there is a time to show that client feedback is taken seriously and acted upon, this is it.

Wrapping up interviews with clarity and confidence

People remember the beginning and end of an experience more vividly than what happens in between. So how do you wrap up on a high?

When you've reached the last of your set questions you should summarise your understanding of what the interviewee has told you. This can be done in a few short sentences. For example: 'That's the last of my questions. What I'm taking away from this is that, overall, you are very satisfied with the service to date: the team has been responsive and courteous, the advice has saved you time, and you feel assured of the technical points. The main area for improvement we've talked about is the accompanying documentation – the errors you discovered that took time to rectify. Greater accuracy in that would help the firm get a higher score next time. Is that a fair reflection of what we've discussed – is there anything we haven't covered or anything to add?'

This approach does two things. First of all, it shows that you have listened and understood. This offers reassurance that their time isn't being wasted. Secondly, it gives the interviewee the opportunity to correct you if you've got something wrong. They can shape the message you take back to the firm.

You might be told yes, that's right – but the thing that *really* matters is this other point. Sometimes you think you're done, but hearing the main points summarised makes the interviewee realise what they missed out. This is another reason you don't want to have rushed the interview and failed to have allowed time for this rounding off – you're not done until you're sure you have the whole picture and the interviewee confirms they're happy with the narrative you're taking away.

In some instances, you won't have a neat little summary like the example above; there will be a long list of problems encountered and things to address. In such instances you want the interviewee on the same side of the table as yourself, to collaborate on the next steps. Ask them which they see as priorities for change, what they would ideally like to see happen next. Very often, the fixes are not things the firm can undertake in isolation – they need the client to work on it with them.

Finally, you should explain the next steps and what to expect, complete with timeline. This will vary depending on what the firm's procedures are, but usually you'll outline how you'll write up your notes and return them to the firm, and inform them that the relevant partner will be in touch to discuss their feedback and the areas for improvement.

Best practices for producing clear and actionable interview transcripts

During the interview you'll take notes continuously as your interviewee speaks. In doing so, you'll capture many false starts and trailing sentences, note things down in cryptic abbreviations, and you'll make countless typos. It will look a mess on the page and most of it will only make sense to you, the notetaker.

The key thing in turning this jumble into a comprehensible and insightful transcript is to write it up as soon as possible. The quality of your report deteriorates the longer you delay. The problem is, having just spent perhaps an hour or more intently listening and engaged, you are mentally and physically tired. You need a break and you should take one. Go and make your hot beverage before going any further.

Your write-up is best done in three sweeps. First, go through it and tidy up: correct the spelling errors, expand on anything abbreviated, delete anything obviously irrelevant. Do this sweep in order to get the distracting bits out of the way so that you can then focus on the content.

Your second sweep needs a higher mental gear. You want to ensure that you have captured the interviewee's words as closely as possible but that the irrelevant parts are left out. Most people are amazed to see a raw transcript of their own words and realise that their speech is full of false starts, *um's* and *ah's*, sentences that trail off without conclusion, and so on. Use your judgement to decide where there should be paragraphs to make the content easier to read.

In most cases, your own words as interviewer can be excluded except where they are essential to continuity and logic. That can be so that the interviewee's words make sense (as when they are referring to something you mentioned), but sometimes it's also important to demonstrate that you raised an issue, that it wasn't necessarily top of their mind. Your prompts may have influenced or led to an idea that might not otherwise have been raised. Where you do retain your own words, surround them in square brackets to make the distinction between yours and the interviewee's.

Your third sweep is simply for proofreading. Your edits will likely have introduced errors. If there's no urgency to return the transcript, then it helps to leave at least a few hours between the second and third sweep. Use a grammar and spelling checker but also reread the transcript thoroughly until you're satisfied it is an accurate record of your conversation.

Always produce an executive summary to accompany each interview transcript

Your interview transcript will be several pages long and run to a few thousand words. You can pass it on and hope that any recipient will discern the key points. Much better is to add a concise executive summary with recommendations: it's likely to be read by more people than the transcript itself.

It will also prove useful to you at later points in time when revisiting it. For example, at the aggregated analysis stage when you are collating the main themes across the sample. Or a year later, when you have a batch of 50 to review and you don't have time to reread each one.

From the interview wrap-up, you'll already have in mind the main points and key message, having paraphrased it back to the interviewee. A good summary is more than this, though. It's first a quick point of reference with the key facts, but it's also your opportunity to interpret the facts and help the firm take action. In this sense, it is more powerful than the transcript itself and so worth spending time on and getting right.

The aim is to have all the key points on one page as clearly and concisely as possible. Writing in bullet points both keeps your thinking tight and makes it easy for the reader to understand. In terms of structure, a few subheadings help group related ideas. A simple but effective structure is to organise as a SWOT analysis with headings for Strengths, Weaknesses, Opportunities, and Threats. Alternatively, you could organise according to the interview topics which might be something like Buying Decision, Service Experience, Competitor Comparisons, Financials.

In selecting what to include, work through the question-naire by section or question, with one or two points each that reflect the conversation and its most salient points. What you choose to exclude is information in itself – something was a non-issue for the interviewee. What you explain in more detail will tend to be the point that was more significant, and which needs driving home.

You should also use the summary to flag what appeared in between the lines – the tone and attitude of the interviewee, where it is in any way remarkable. The level of enthusiasm and praise isn't always apparent in a transcript, so it helps to say if the interviewee was gushing in their compliments. Likewise, the question that caused them to roll their eyes – you'll need to convey that sense of exasperation or disbelief because otherwise it won't be apparent from the transcription itself. The transcript is all facts but the summary is there to include interpretation and direction.

Write recommendations that lead to immediate business transformation

With some interviews, the summary alone will make the next steps glaringly obvious. The partner or others working on the account will recognise what is critical to act on right away and what can be left until later. As the interviewer, it's hard to always know what will resonate with someone close to the relationship. Either way, you should spell out what you think is needed: you should add a selection of suggested actions or recommenda-tions. Whether these are then acted upon or ignored doesn't matter – you are offering a choice of starting points to work from.

You'll normally have points for improvement at two levels tactical account level and then broader strategy level that applies beyond just this client. It can help to break these out under separate headings if you know that they'll be relayed on via separate channels to the account team and to leadership respectively.

With both types, you need to strike a balance between being specific and clear in what you think needs to happen but, given that you don't necessarily know the resources available and other priorities present, leave the specifics and the decision to those in the business responsible for applying the changes.

Very basic tactical recommendations can be taking the interviewee off or adding them onto a mailing list. It can be suggesting a follow up meeting to discuss training and development support. Pretty uncontentious and straightforward stuff. It gets tricky with knotty issues. For example, where there are problems with the quality of work delivered by a specific individual, or ardent objections to fees and invoices.

With more contentious issues, don't jump to conclusions, don't blame anyone, and don't over-egg problems. If a solution isn't obvious or it's not appropriate for us to propose one, then simply reflect the situation and flag that it needs investigating. The recommendation might be to explore a grievance – setting up a meeting to progress it may be enough at the initial stage. Flagging it to be addressed so that it is not overlooked is an important step because, too often, feedback is given and ignored, which undermines relationships and faith in the feedback exercise.

Generally, tactical recommendations are ones where there is often a relatively quick fix solution or at least it's clear where to start. Strategy-level recommendations may not be easy to address but that doesn't mean you should shy away from making them. For example, if the firm can't expect any additional work for a particular practice or in a geography because it lacks the reputation for capability there, it's probably a wider firm issue. Opening a new office in a foreign territory isn't going to happen off the back of your interview, but if it's a known issue that leadership is considering then there is value in it being recorded. We shouldn't assume that a bold recommendation is frivolous – we are raising the issue for others to decide and act on as they see fit.

On the whole, where you can, be very specific about recommended actions. However, where you don't know what the best solution will be but the account owner likely will, just highlight the issue to be resolved (the what), not necessarily the method (the how) to be employed.

Takeaways

- To get open and candid feedback, use someone independent of the relationship to conduct your feedback interviews (from a different department or practice, but ideally an independent third party).

- Keep interviews as one-to-one interactions wherever possible – you'll get more candid conversations that are easier to record.

- Get a personal briefing from the relationship owner in advance, in order to understand the work, relationship, and any personalities and politics to be aware of.

- Don't record the audio of your interviews – it inhibits some interviewees and generates too much verbal waste; have your interviewers learn to touch-type to a good standard instead.

- Interviewers should set out expectations at the beginning: thank the interviewee, explain the purpose of the exercise (including how a questionnaire is used and the duration).

- Follow the questionnaire but don't be a slave to it: be flexible and let the conversation flow naturally; interviews should be stimulating and enjoyable.

- Interviewers should use additional probing questions to explore and understand the interviewee's priorities beneath the surface – unlike with surveys, you can go off-piste to gather the most valuable insights.

- Wrap up with a summary that shows you've understood the main messages, then explain the next steps, demonstrating that this has been a good use of their time and that you are committed to closing-the-loop.

- Produce interview transcripts as close to verbatim as possible but leave out the waffle and niceties; always include an executive summary at the front-end with clear and practical action points for account-level improvement.

CHAPTER 6
HOW TO DESIGN AND DEPLOY ONLINE SURVEYS

I keep six honest serving-men
(They taught me all I knew);
Their names are What and Why and When
And How and Where and Who.

—Rudyard Kipling

Lavish them with top-notch hospitality? Kidnap and hold their loved ones to ransom? There's no denying it's a challenge to get busy executives to take the time to fill in a survey. Fortunately, there are easier carrot and stick approaches to persuading people to not only participate but to be generous with their judgement and opinions. Incentives matter but so does managing expectations to guarantee not only repeat custom, but a continuous stream of future feedback too.

Surveys are an out-of-date technology... but they still work

Surveys are old hat, passé, from a bygone era of standing in the street with a clipboard. Everyone hates them and nobody fills them in. That's the typically sniffy sentiment that's common, and it's no surprise when you can't even use a public lavatory without being asked to rate your experience via electronic display.

Yet, more surveys are sent and completed than ever before due to the ease and effectiveness of online surveying. Surveys are an irritation when they are either badly timed, ask about irrelevancies, or require an amount of effort incommensurate with the transaction completed.

Without wishing to get too highfalutin about it, surveys can be wonderful devices for emotional release. As human beings, when we are delighted we want to share our experience and credit the source of that pleasure. When we are vexed, we want a means to vent our anger. Surveys provide that emotional outlet. You don't get much opportunity for cathartic release in business, but the modest survey delivers.

Make your survey questions easy to answer, especially your opening ones

Asking questions is easy; the challenge is asking questions that get you powerful insights while requiring the minimum of effort from respondents. Many people starting out in research try to cram in too many questions in an effort to be as comprehensive as possible, and in doing so thrust the unsuspecting respondent into a mind-numbing maze of despair. If they do escape it, they'll never willingly re-enter it again. That's a disaster because we want their feedback on a continuous basis – we want to track sentiment over time, and so we need to sustain goodwill, not undermine all the positive experiences they have engaging with your actual service.

'Evil' long surveys tend to come with mysterious questions. It's tempting to write lengthy questions that explain every possible interpretation of a question in detail. However, anything more than a line of text is too much. Likewise, there can be a temptation to write clever questions that make you look impressive in front of senior colleagues who might review them, but 'clever' questions tend to be hard to answer. It's not about showing off; it's about eliciting the best possible answer.

Instead, write using plain and simple language that assumes no specialist knowledge. Cut out every non-essential word to make it as easy a task as possible. The tone of writing should match your brand's voice rather than the type of language you use in your technical documents. Informal yet polite is usually best.

For relationship surveys, you want to capture the overall state of the relationship between the individual and your firm. Net Promoter Score is the best headline metric for a relationship survey because it will help you gauge loyalty and future buying intent. The other core questions should take a snapshot of the client experience across a range of service dimensions and relationship measures. Questions on the commercial elements of the relationship belong in this sort of survey too – value for money, budget management, or fee levels.

Your choice of questions beyond these will depend on what's on your firm's agenda at present. Topics might include added-value activities, current business challenges, pressing regulatory changes, priorities around environmental, social and governance matters, brand perception, or others subjects of a horizon-scanning nature.

By contrast, transactional surveys are conducted as soon as possible after a distinct client interaction has ended. The questions are less about the overall relationship with the firm and more about the most recent experience – the touchpoints encountered as part of the matter or project.

In terms of time to complete (and therefore type and number of questions to ask), relationship surveys should generally take no more than about 10 minutes to complete and ideally, less. Transactional ones should be even shorter, at around the two to five minute marker. Before launching, you can get an initial estimate of completion times by asking colleagues to complete the survey, substituting your firm's performance for a recent service interaction they've had. For example, thinking about the bank they use. They'll need to use their imagination a little, but many elements of service such as responsiveness, communication, and attitude are universal.

Once you have a survey live – and ideally as part of a small-scale pilot before the main launch – you can track completion times via your survey software to gauge whether you've got this right or not. Depending on your provider, you should also be able to see where survey abandonments occur, to further help you diagnose weak questions or where you've overstayed your welcome in terms of attention span.

Types of question influence engagement and completion times

Minimising the number of questions you ask is not the only means of ensuring high levels of engagement and completion rates. The type of question you ask is critical too. Self-administered online surveys are best suited to gathering structured data – the simple scoring and rating stuff. Of course, on its own, that information doesn't tell the whole story you want to capture –

whatever the rating, you want to know the *why* behind it too. So, for this reason, there's a little psychology to the survey journey. It is simple, though.

Start your survey with closed-ended ratings questions that are easy to answer. Not that they should be about trivial subjects but visibly straightforward enough to answer that respondents get past the first screen. Abandonment rates are highest at the very first question when the first question demands a long essay-style answer. We want deep insights but not on the first page. If we can get people past the first question, then the more they complete, the increasingly incentivised they are to reach the end and hit 'submit'. For this reason, as far as is logical in your survey flow, hold back your open-ended questions until near the end. Until that point, the only open-ended answer containers should be optional comments boxes for those who want to add a little word or two of explanation to their ratings. It's especially useful to have these at the pilot stage because early respondents will point out if an option is missing or something is unclear. The survey gods love pedants.

Among ratings questions, the main subtypes are: semantic (e.g. Excellent – Poor); numeric (e.g. 1-5); Likert (e.g. Strongly Agree – Strongly Disagree); semantic frequency (e.g. Always – Never); and rank (putting a set of attributes into order). Besides these, the other common closed-ended type you have are simply multiple-choice and binary-choice selections.

The type you deploy depends on your objective, what you want to learn, and what will best capture it. However, if you want to make responding quicker and easier, put questions of the same type together – your respondents become accustomed to a repeated scale, and so they are easy to skim through. Too many, though, and it becomes a monotonous chore and so having more than one type helps keep things interesting. Once you're up to the halfway mark, use more of the open-ended questions because at that point you're more guaranteed engagement. In summary, use *variety* for interest and *consistency* for speed.

With all these questions, take care to mete out both sides of the scale evenly and with balanced terms: a 'strongly agree' on one side needs a 'strongly disagree' on the other. Use terms that are commonly accepted as opposites. It's not as easy as you may initially think: 'fast' versus 'slow' is straightforward, but what's the opposite of 'excellent'? Is it merely 'poor' or should it be 'awful', or even 'terrible'? Should you have a midpoint (for example, 'neither agree nor disagree') or force a stance one way or the other? There are arguments for not offering a neutral selection, but – generally – having a midpoint is the safe option, keeping everyone on board.

Perhaps conspicuous by their absence are demographic lines of questioning – at least, getting their name and email address. They're often the first things in a questionnaire, so why not in your survey? These are supposed to be your clients – you live to serve them; their fees put food on the table. Why would you torment them by asking for information you already hold in your database?! Names, email addresses, their inside leg measurements, and other relevant information that connects their survey responses back to their entries in your CRM system should be invisibly seeded at the point they click on your survey request. There's nothing more frustrating than having to repeat information your service provider already knows.

There's also an added benefit in that by not having to enter that information it's less front of mind how their responses are attributable back to them. As a result, they tend to be more candid. We're talking at a subconscious level – they will have had at least two explanations at the point of starting to answer questions that the survey is NOT anonymous and the reason being that the firm will implement improvements at account level, based on the feedback provided.

Use question routing for a slick respondent experience

Having insisted that you know your client and so you should save them time in avoiding unnecessary questions, here's a bit of leeway that's allowed. In theory, you also know the service lines they've instructed, who worked on particular matters, what the fees were, and a range of other useful information. No doubt it does all exist, but is it in the same system, a system that talks to the other systems and is reliably up to date? No? You're not alone. And for that reason, there will be elements you want feedback on that potentially you could prepopulate into the survey and route them on that basis. For example, they use services *x, y, z,* and so there's no need to ask for ratings of *a, b, c.* If you trust your data then great, do it. But otherwise get your respondent to select the type of work or the offices they interact with – those sorts of usage markers which can be insightful for you to have if you don't have them on record. From there, you can show them only the questions that relate to their relationship with the firm.

Target participants need heads-up contact before the survey itself goes out

You've got your survey ready; how do we get clients there? The key to healthy response rates is having the client's primary point of contact at the firm be the person to make the request – as personalised an entreaty as possible. Don't be tempted to rely on the official account manager or relationship partner – you want the person they actually know and work with; seniority is irrelevant for this.

An email from someone trusted does several things. It prepares the individual, setting the expectation that a further request is coming so it won't be out of the blue. It helps connect the firm with the survey software provider or research partner in the client's mind, so the name is that bit more familiar, providing reassurance that this isn't an elaborate phishing scam from an unknown company. It also provides an additional touchpoint that can reinforce or help rekindle the commercial relationship, which is especially useful during a relatively fallow period common to project-based work. It's surprising the number of times a partner reveals that their email about the survey prompted their client to respond, saying they'd been meaning to get in touch and arranging to meet over something upcoming.

If partners can be sufficiently engaged and persuaded, then they might even go so far as to pick up the phone and alert the client in that even more personalised manner. A nudge from the partner is often all it takes.

For annual relationship surveys – particularly the first time you conduct one – you want to emphasise to clients how this is really important; it's not a boring compliance tick-the-box task. Rather, the client team will be on tenterhooks, repeatedly clicking refresh, desperate to hear the client's verdict on their performance of late!

Great invitation copy will get you great response rates

Your survey might be a thing of beauty, full of thought-provoking questions that will uncover original insights from the depths of your respondents' minds. Except, you won't get any of that unless you can persuade them to drop whatever activity they are set on doing and switch attention to your survey.

Your email copy conveying respondents to the survey needs to be more than a nice polite request to complete the survey: it needs to be a compelling opportunity worth investing time in. It needs to make it very clear what respondents need to do, and what the payoff will be for taking the time to do it. Good email copy is key to response rates.

So, what are the main ingredients to get great response rates? Let's start super-basic: get their name right and get the URL right. Is the combination of your database and mailing system capable of seeding those two elements correctly? This isn't a facetious point – you often see these basics incorrectly seeded in marketing comms, and by the time you correct it and send a second mailing you've already knocked 30 per cent off your response rate, regardless of everything else you do.

Levelling up from here, your email copy has to look and feel legitimate. People are rightly suspicious of emails asking them to go and click on links to third-party websites and hand over information about themselves. Good IT systems will screen and intervene on their behalf so they never even get sight of your email. Therefore, you must demonstrate that this is a safe email from a trusted source and not a phishing scam. If the email isn't coming directly from your firm's address, then use the firm's name in the subject line. In your salutation, use whatever is normal – if most communications start with 'Hi Joe', don't switch to 'Dear Mr Doe' for this exercise.

The most convincing tactic of all is to refer to the client's main point of contact at the firm in the first line. Something along the lines of, 'Your relationship partner, Jo Doe, has asked for your feedback on how well the firm is meeting your expectations in terms of service delivery and value for money'. It has to be a name they know and trust. You may use the firm's head honcho because surely everyone knows who Jamie is? Well, not everyone knows, cares or remembers your managing partner – it's not personal enough. Unless that partner is the person they work with day in and day out, who told them about this feedback exercise, then you haven't gone personal enough.

For some firms, there isn't necessarily an undisputed account owner. Seeding the names of half a dozen different individuals looks a bit silly, and trying to get consensus on who should be named on these emails isn't worth your time. An alternative which works for post-transaction surveys in particular is to reference the matter name. This is likely to be instantly recognisable even if it is a bit long-winded or enigmatic in the case of confidential deals.

The last element in passing the sniff test is this: don't mask your survey URL with words like 'click here'. It makes the email more likely to be filtered out by automated spam detection and doesn't feel safe to click on for a human either. If the URL is short and makes sense when read, use it as it is. For example, www.lawfirm.com/feedback doesn't look like it's masquerading as something else. However, if it's an unfathomably long link then substitute some friendly text like Complete the Feedback Survey Here. In addition, you can share that full unmasked link somewhere at the bottom of your email where it can be copied and pasted, should the link itself be disabled.

Having dealt with the hygiene factors, what is going to get that click-through? You are really answering two questions: Why me and why now? You have to give reasons and benefits for filling in the survey, otherwise your respondent can assume someone else (a colleague, for example) can take care of this. Or else they decide they'll come back to it some other time… and won't.

If you've decided that you'll incentivise your survey – with a reward of some sort, such as a donation to a charity – then that's a straightforward reason, albeit an extrinsic rather than intrinsic reward. Other motivators are simply setting out the fact that the firm or the partner genuinely wants feedback in order to improve, that they want to foster a culture of continuous improvement, and that this in turn will contribute to the service that clients receive in future.

Even better is to explain with some detail how the scores and comments will be used – who will review them and when. If the managing partner will read each one, if the findings will be used at board level, if the feedback will be shared (anonymously) at the upcoming partner conference, then this shows that the comments won't just get filed away and forgotten about.

For some people, that's motivating – if they are invested in the firm overall, and want to see it grow and succeed. Not everyone cares, though, and so an emphasis on change for their direct benefit matters more. In which case, explain how the account team will review the feedback together and devise specific account-level improvements. Add what form the follow-up will take. For large accounts where many people from the same organisation are surveyed, will there be a report that gets shared with their boss? For some, that will mean there is both carrot and stick, making them feel more obligated to contribute.

If you've included sector specific questions (of the thought leadership variety) then offering to share anonymous findings where respondents get to see the opinion of their peers can be encouraging. Any sort of report – a tangible output from the exercise – can be an incentive, because it demonstrates that there will be acknowledgement and action from the firm.

When asked why they didn't take part in a feedback exercise, the most common reason is that the target respondent simply didn't think it would make any difference. People are used to filling out forms that they never hear about again. We have to convince people that we are serious about listening, that their contribution will be recognised, and that change will result.

Doing so, of course, sets expectations around follow-up, so we need to be realistic about what can be achieved. Remember not to overpromise what the outcomes will be, or you'll disappoint. Consequently, response rates in future will be worse because you haven't delivered in the past.

This extends as far as giving an estimated completion time. Telling someone it's a two-minute survey means they will likely do it there and then. If it's a 15-minute investment, they're likely to mark it and put it to one side to return to later. Obviously, the shorter the timeframe, the more likely you are to get a response. What's important is to ensure that your estimate is roughly correct. There is nothing more maddening that to find the progress bar hasn't budged after 10 minutes into a supposedly two-minute survey. Do not bait and switch.

Besides legitimacy, incentivisation, and expectation management, what else will help?

Email subject lines should be distinctive in terms of what the exercise is, so that it doesn't get confused with marketing junk. This is a 'Client Service Review' for instance – making it a formal part of the service itself, not a 'nice to have' extra – rather than 'Tell us your opinion', which can be ignored without consequence.

You can add urgency by including closing dates. You might offer a minor reward for the first 100 responses received, for instance. However, this can undermine what you've set out: if you've emphasised how important the feedback is, then suddenly wanting rapid responses (rather than well considered thoughtful input) can appear contradictory.

Formatting can help in a number of ways: underlining key information for emphasis, putting other parts in bold, and generally spacing things out to be as readable as possible. This matters because while you may write copy as though people will read it, in most cases it only gets scanned for the most the pertinent details. For example, making it easy to find the link to click on by having it sit on a line of its own is a simple but effective way of increasing response rates.

The last step, having drafted your email copy: now edit down the text until it's half the length you began with (in terms of word count), and then double the number of paragraphs you've used. If you've signposted the email correctly in terms of simple messages, reassuring recognisable elements, and put it in an easy-to-follow format, then they won't read it in a conscious way; they'll absorb it at a glance and click through immediately.

Always send a reminder request (or two) but nagging is counterproductive

Having crafted a persuasive and compelling invitation email, don't stop there. Getting really high response rates depends on following up. You get the bulk of responses from your initial email but a sizeable number from reminders. The law of diminishing returns does apply, so there are limits to how effective reminders are, but typically you can expect to get about 60 per cent of responses from your first mailing, 30 per cent from a first reminder, and the remaining 10 per cent from your last attempt.

With a few exceptions, it's usually a mistake to send more than this: it gets annoying for recipients, you look desperate, and it reduces the goodwill of otherwise happy clients who just happen to not wish to take part. All for just a few more responses.

Reminders should be gentle both in terms of message and frequency. Setting reminders to go out on a weekly schedule is most effective. You're not going to convince every recipient to take part; it's the people who are willing but busy who you're trying to get on board. You know how it is when you're up against a deadline with a heavy workload: a survey from anyone is not a priority, and you may not even bother to mark it as something to come back to later. If you're out of office on holiday, it's going to wait until you have time. This is why a mailing, followed by two reminders each with a week's interval, works – because over a three-week period people will return from holiday, or get through whatever else has occupied them, and they'll find the time. Sending a reminder out indefinitely every couple of days will just create irate clients.

It also helps to set expectations around the schedule: you can tell your target respondents that they'll receive a reminder in seven days' time. You can tell them how many reminders they'll receive. And, importantly, provide an opt-out link that allows them to unsubscribe from the mailings. Don't hide it either – make it clear that the option is there so that the recipient is in control.

Another way to improve the effectiveness of your reminder emails is to vary the copy you use. The reminder doesn't necessarily need to include as much detail as the original. Shorter emails get more responses because they are easier to scan and decide to act upon.

A good reminder email should reference the previous email, explain the purpose of the survey and supply the link – without any waffle.

Depending on the tone of voice your brand adopts, going light-hearted in nudging people toward completing can extract many more responses than repetitive, dry, and formal wording.

This is particularly effective when combined with personalisation of the messaging. If you have the individuals' details and the partners', use these to the best effect: joke that the partner is sweating, or waiting with bated breath to find out the ratings the client gives. Despite including their name and point of contact, people know that it's a template email they're receiving but the levity is still appreciated. A little surprise can unlock the willingness to spare a few minutes to respond.

Prepare to deal with these common enquiries

Despite your best efforts to anticipate all your clients' needs and possible queries, there will be people who need clarification, who get confused, who run into technical problems, or other issues. If you've got a team around you or you're using a research partner, then the good news is these are not your problems. Otherwise, here's a heads-up of the most common type of reactions, enquiries, and requests that come up, along with suggested ways to deal with them. Usually, they come via email, unless you've included a phone number for support (which is best practice).

This isn't a good time

It probably would have been quicker for them to fill in the survey than tell you that they're too busy. Nonetheless, acknowledge that, pause mailings, and let them know you'll reactive it in x number of weeks.

I'm not the right person

With luck, they've told you who *is* the right person, and so you can cross-reference your client list and substitute in the person they've nominated instead.

I'll tell you what I think...

Some people want to give you feedback but don't want to fill in a survey – they're technophobic, or else have something to express they don't feel is best done electronically. Go through the questions with them over the phone; they'll appreciate you making the effort to do so, and you'll capture better insights.

My company is blocking your link

Some businesses can be overly cautious with their firewalls and anti-phishing protection – financial institutions in particular – so include an unmasked version of the URL. Worst case scenario, supply the survey as an attachment instead, or – like with the previous and they've called you – just take their answers over the phone.

Expedite any bad news and problem cases

Besides direct queries about the survey itself, you need to be prepared to respond rapidly to clients who report any sort of acute service failure. Clients who are extremely unhappy or disappointed have often taken the time to tell you about the situation in the hope that doing so might rescue the relationship. It's important to heed these cries immediately, rather than wait to process and go through your closing-the-loop motions in the usual fashion (which while effective may take weeks and leaves your unhappy client stewing in the meantime).

If you have only a trickle of survey responses coming back to you, it may be that you keep an eye out for these, glancing over them as they arrive in your inbox or reporting console. However, you can't do this once your programme reaches any significant scale.

The solution is to set conditional alerts in your survey software that trigger an email based on one or more survey variables being selected. The most common is one that has logic along the lines of: 'If NPS rating is less than or equal to six, send an email to this address'. This way, you get to know every time you get a detractor response and can review it to determine if action is required. That might still generate more alerts than you personally want to deal with on a day-to-day basis, so you can combine it with other data (for example, client spend at a particular threshold, so that you only need react when it is a high-value client that is at risk of defecting).

To take yourself out of the equation entirely, you can set your protocols such that red flag alerts go to the relevant individuals in the business to be dealt with. For example, heads of sectors receive those originating from their clients. Or, you take a topic-specific approach and, for instance, low ratings of your technology platform cause someone in your IT department to be pinged in order for them to investigate.

One other option to consider is enabling survey respondents to initiate the triage process themselves. For those providing ratings that indicate out-of-the-ordinary levels of dissatisfaction, you can route them to a question that acknowledges those low scores and asks them if they'd like a call to help resolve the issue You can give them a range of options about who should contact them, so they are in charge of the escalation – is it their relationship partner, an independent party, the managing partner? Adding this sort of function demonstrates how seriously you take ensuring high performance in service delivery and relationship management. Of course, in doing so you are also setting the expectation that you will make every effort to fix things quickly; meaning any failure to do so will only exacerbate the initial problem. This means higher stakes, but it's also much more impressive when you manage to fulfil that promise.

Iterate and improve over time to get better response rates

Response rates are a sign of two things. First, how engaged your clients are in general (a good open-rate is a sign of relationship health in itself) and second, the quality of your survey. The latter is dependent on creating an engaging and enjoyable experience. Stimulating, thought-provoking, but not overly demanding questions do this.

You can use data on open-rates, points of abandonment, and completion duration to help you refine and improve your surveys. A good research partner should give you a great head start on this but it can, equally, be learned through gradual refinement over time.

Takeaways

- Making your opening questions easy to answer – tick-box format rather than more demanding open-ended ones – gets more people started and more responses completed.

- Keep it short: run a pilot and record completion times to see how well your questionnaire is working, then prune and revise questions.

- Repeating a question format makes it easier and quicker for respondents to answer, but you also need variety to keep it interesting and keep respondents engaged.

- Seed information you already have so you avoid annoying respondents by asking obvious questions. Also, use routing to tailor the survey experience to every respondent.

- Coordinate your communications from relationship partner to survey provider to avoid getting filtered out as junk or ignored as unimportant – it should look and feel like a personal request, not a mass mailing.

- Send tailored reminders to non-responders to increase your response rate, but don't exceed more than a couple of nudges or you risk being annoying.

- Expedite bad news to those who can address it best, rather than wait for longer closing-the-loop processes to take care of client concerns.

- Iterate your question sets and email copy to gradually improve engagement and response rates over time.

CHAPTER 7
ANALYSIS AND REPORTING: ORGANISING AND COMMUNICATING ACTIONABLE INSIGHTS

Data are just summaries of thousands of stories – tell a few of those stories to help make the data meaningful.

—Chip and Dan Heath

Data get stored away in files and folders in directories, unread and long forgotten about. There's far too much data and too little time, so it can be tempting to settle for surface-level learnings. Skipping analysis is always a mistake though, because it's the only means of converting data into insight. It's worthwhile because insights are what unlock the solutions to impossible problems, drive change, revolutionise business models, and disrupt markets.

Why analyse and report at an aggregated level?

The purpose of analysis and reporting is to first understand and then disseminate information. Feedback must be made clear and easy to comprehend, as well as easy to share with everyone involved in client success.

The most basic level of this is to make feedback available client by client in a question-answer format, whether from online survey or personal interview. There's no aggregation or interpretation; it's the client voice and nothing else. This is useful in itself and shouldn't be overlooked but you need to do more work in order to spot underlying patterns and trends in the responses to really get transformational benefits from the feedback.

Software does not do the job of analysis for you

Once you've set up a survey and used it to collect responses, you have your insights at individual respondent or client level and you can begin to act on account-level improvements. But how do you get the wider operational and strategic insights? It's by conducting aggregated analysis.

For some, analysis is equated with special software and fancy charts. And it's true that most research software will spit out a range of frequency tables and charts. But analysis is foremost about having a clear set of objectives in mind while exploring data, comparing and contrasting information to identify patterns and trends, then interpreting these as observations that are meaningful in a business context. Some questions you begin with and find answers to immediately; others emerge only gradually as you peel back layers, revealing hidden drivers and underlying causes of the phenomenon you observe.

Understand the types of data that can be collected

Your aim may be to get deep operational insights and penetrating strategic revelations, but where you begin is with a confounding mound of data.

Broadly speaking, data can be divided into two types: unstructured and structured. The unstructured comes care of open-ended questions that allow free-form answers. This data is valuable in and of itself at an account level, but to be exploited at aggregated level it needs converting into a form of structured data, whereby it can be counted. Structured data branches out into two main types: categorical and quantifiable. You have descriptive and ranked within the categorical bucket (stats professionals may prefer 'nominal' and 'ordinal' terminology), and continuous and discrete within the quantifiable one.

Categorical data can't be measured numerically but it can be classified into sets; you can tally the counts of each category. Quantifiable data can be measured numerically – each data value can be assigned a position on a numerical scale. Quantifiable data can be continuous and discrete. Continuous data can take any value, while discrete data is limited to the options you've provided, say, on a scale of one to 10.

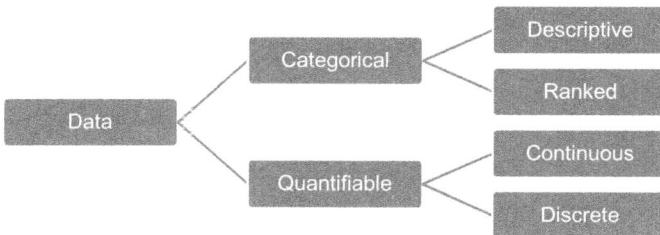

Convert open-ended answers into themes by coding the comments

While the structured data is ready to go for analysis, the unstructured stuff needs some transforming to begin with.

Online surveys tend to produce short statements that are easy to interpret. 'The documents had lots of errors in them' might be the explanation for a low rating given in relation to 'quality'. By contrast, personal interviews produce masses of text passages. A single interview transcript, documenting an hour's conversation, can easily run to five or six thousand words. They are rich, containing a multitude of topics and ideas, but there will also be swathes of superfluous information – various digressions that came up in the natural flow of conversation. This makes it more difficult to cajole into a useful form.

Surely, in this day and age there's no need to read it all though? That depends. Building on artificial intelligence and large language modelling technologies, text analytics programmes exist that can be trained to code and classify comments incredibly quickly and efficiently. The accuracy is still not always there, though, so your choice of human or machine comes down to the volume of data you need to process and the accuracy of outputs that you require.

For very large volume B2C usage in fairly simple fields, the machines have it sewn up. A hotel chain receiving tens of thousands of responses just needs the machine to pick out the term 'wi-fi' and then determine the associated sentiment based on the language used, and it can interpret that there was a problem with the wi-fi connectivity.

For professional services, there tends to be a lot more nuance to the text outputs we gather, and so it's more that we are on the cusp of a revolution, but not quite there yet. It may give you a head start, but either you or your team will need to roll up sleeves and get stuck into the data. For example, your text analytics tool might scan a transcript and summarise the entire content and make recommendations in seconds, but they still look a bit like this:

The client: (1) Is satisfied overall with service quality (2) Had a lovely time on holiday last week (3) Is moderately pleased with the fee levels incurred.

In other words, this sort of tech needs training in what does and doesn't matter to you. Even then, it's still poor at discriminating whenever it encounters something outside its training.

Again, if you have huge volumes of feedback data, it will be a necessity to adopt the machine approach to analysing free-form text answers for your aggregated analysis. However, for much of the time firms only run personal interviews with a limited sample of the most valuable clients and so, rather than utilise shiny new software, a more traditional approach is optimal.

For a person tasked with dealing with your unstructured, open-ended comment data, the goal is to identify the main themes and group comments according to those themes, thus making your data structured and readily available for quantitative analysis. This task is usually called 'coding' which has nothing to do with computer programming, apart from the need to think and work in a very logical and methodical manner.

As the comment coder, you take a sample of comments – between about 10 and 20 per cent of the total amount you have to work with – and read each one, assigning a code or theme to each comment. In doing so, you compile a codebook that should include each code, its definition, and an example. You need your codes to be very clearly defined so that if another person takes over from you they will code consistently with your set of terms. Deciding what should constitute a distinct code may take more than one sweep of your sample data. A good criterion for coding is that your themes should be MECE (mutually exclusive, collectively exhaustive). This approach tries to eliminate any overlap or duplication.

Generally speaking, a manageable number of codes is around 20 to 30 distinct themes. Many more than this, and it becomes too difficult to hold the library of codes in your mind. Less than that, and your analysis lacks the granularity to reveal anything useful.

Once your codebook is ready, you can code up the entire data set. It's advisable to not only code the theme but also the sentiment, so that as well as knowing something is a hot topic you can also easily recognise if it is for the right or wrong reasons. A positive, neutral, and negative set of categories is sufficient in most cases. This way, you'll be able to create statistics like, 'Overall, 70 per cent of respondents describe a positive experience with using our meeting rooms', rather than just saying 70 per cent *mention* meeting rooms.

This human approach to thematic text coding is far better at interpreting nuanced or ambiguous conversation found in interview transcripts than machines. It is, however, very hard to scale because it depends on knowledgeable individuals doing a manual task and so becomes expensive for larger volumes of data.

Human or machine, once text is in a structured format then you are all set to crunch the numbers.

There are three steps to analysis: statement, comparison, and regression

Your research fieldwork has reaped masses of data that needs converting into insights, by means of analysis. There are generally three phases in this transformation.

First is *stating* the evidence – setting it out in a comprehendible form, usually a series of tables with the frequencies at which each variable occurs. You want a simple tally with which you can see the lay of the land. Many things become immediately apparent about the population you've surveyed – you can see overall score distributions, what is popular, what's a source of irritation, and so on – simply by looking at what's highest or lowest rated. The limitation is that there is no nuance; it's everybody's view all at once, and all the detail is hidden.

Second comes the *compare* phase. This is when you 'cut' the data in different ways, filtering so that you see only a subsection of your respondents at a time. Some of these groupings, or segments, are naturally baked into the information you hold about them or the way you interact with them. For example, geographically you could compare the CSAT scores of clients who are based in one region versus another, or equally, clients who instruct a particular office versus another. Clearly, it doesn't need to be a one-to-one comparison, you can divvy up respondents and compare multiple groupings at once.

Doing so reveals patterns, and by putting results in order you can see strengths and weaknesses. The compare phase is where it starts to get complex because there are, quickly, a vast number of permutations to any cross-tabulation. There isn't necessarily a comprehensive way of cross-comparing all the different respondent fields and answers. Partly it comes down to instincts about what might be interesting to see, or what is linked to the firm's current agenda. The more data you've collected then the bigger the job you've created for yourself.

By this point, you are ready to get into the third phase which is *regression*, employing statistical techniques to reveal connections that aren't identifiable from straightforward observation alone. Different terms get used for this such as 'root cause analysis' or 'driver analysis'. The aim is to identify not only correlation but the direction of causation too.

This is where it can get complex and you might want to involve an expert in statistics. Regression analysis often requires the checking of assumptions (for example, linearity, homoscedasticity, multicollinearity) to ensure the model is valid. If we don't meet the model's assumptions, we need to use alternative models for non-linear or categorical dependent variables (for example, logistic regression or decision trees).

Boiling it all down, we're asking: if we get this particular element of service right or wrong, does it have an impact on the client's other perceptions? Having established that, then does dialling up or down one aspect of your service delivery have an outsized influence on another part? Based on the data you've collected, you hope to be able to model likely buyer behaviour and forecast likely future purchase outcomes.

Firms use this sort of driver analysis to reduce client churn by doing less of the things that cause dissatisfaction and cause clients to leave, and more of the things where there is evidence of them spending larger amounts, more frequently, and over extended periods.

Choose data visualisations based on your audience and objectives

Finally: the sexy stuff! A huge amount of time might go into preparing and tabulating data but to really explain and disseminate our findings, we need to put the information into an easily digestible form. Data visualisation is at an all-time high of popularity, and for good reason. Visuals persuade better and faster than simply telling someone, enabling them to see for themselves. The right visuals – primarily charts – bring feedback to life, grab attention, and motivate people to action.

The best place to start in creating a great visualisation is by asking yourself what it is you want to convey: what is the purpose of each visualisation? You select the form based on its function. Ask: Who is the audience for this? What information do they want to unlock? What questions will that information in turn provoke? And what conversations or actions do we want to occur? The point is that we should anticipate questions and use of the information – the audience for the visual should find it easy to understand and act on the visual's message.

Track trends over time with line, area, and bar charts

One of the most frequently asked questions is simply whether we are improving or deteriorating at delivering a particular aspect of service. Some of the best visuals for showing trends over time are line charts, area charts, and bar charts. Following common cultural convention, you put time on the x-axis and the thing you are measuring on the y-axis. Line charts make information over time fairly clear.

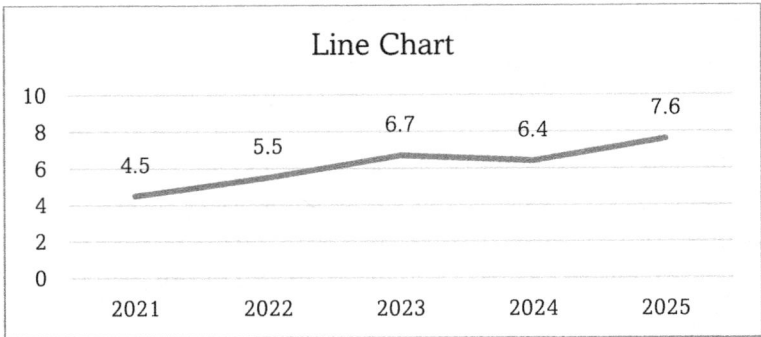

The only limitation is that you can't see how the different elements contribute to the total over time. Using an area chart enables you to see how the elements combine as a single pattern, while a bar chart gives you the individual time periods as single patterns.

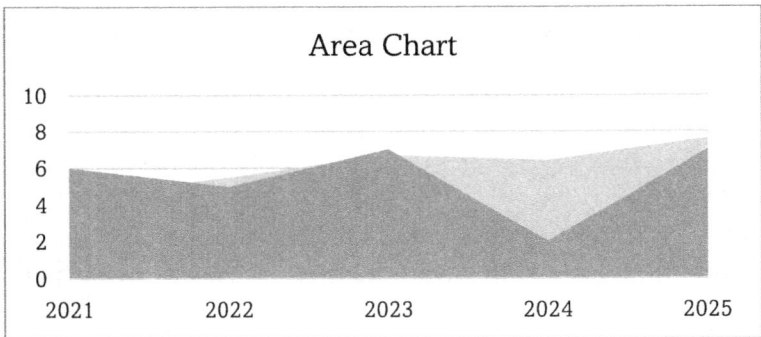

Use bar charts for comparing and ranking

Comparing or ranking subsets of information such as practices, regions, service lines, and so on, is a common need when you want to see relative performance or importance. Good old bar charts are great for comparison because they build in quantitative values as length on the same baseline, making it really easy to compare values.

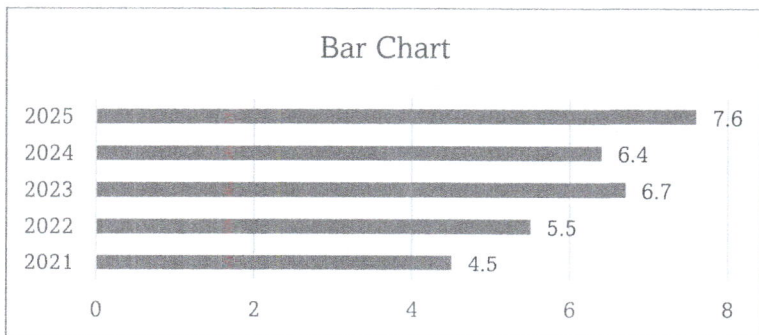

Bar Chart

Year	Value
2025	7.6
2024	6.4
2023	6.7
2022	5.5
2021	4.5

They're not exciting visuals but they are super-practical and functional.

Scatter and bubble charts for correlation, and hopefully, causation too

Once you have your information laid out clearly, your enquiring mind then begins to hypothesise possible relationships between the things measured. You'll wonder about what's inter-related. What's driving client loyalty? Does top-of-mind competitor set influence value for money ratings? Do clients who buy services less frequently rate value-add activities differently to those with an ongoing relationship?

A simple correlation analysis can identify these relationships – potentially, that is. Not necessarily causation, for which you'll need further statistical investigation. But visually, a scatter chart is a clear way of setting this out, complete with a trend line for reference. One level up from this, adding another dimension, is a bubble chart which can be super effective when you introduce revenue, for example, so it becomes apparent how much you might need to worry about poor performance.

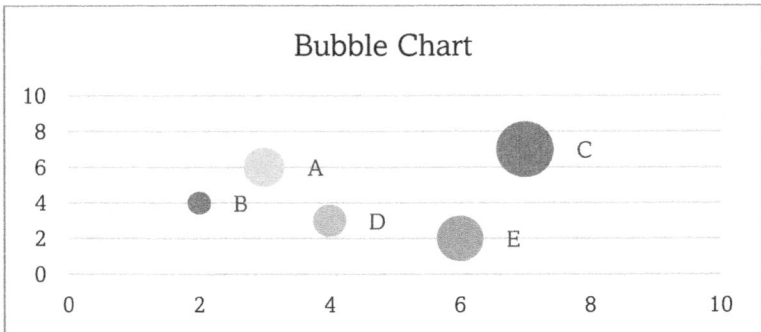

Bubble Chart

Use boxplots to show distribution

Averages are dangerous – especially when sample sizes are relatively small. You've heard how the average disposable income of the people at a party jumps to a few billion when Warren Buffett walks in the room. And so, including distribution within your visualisations is a smart way to offer a sense check to the data you're describing. For this, a box plot may be appropriate as they excel at displaying multiple distributions. They pack all your data points into a box and whisker display. This allows you to see the highest and lowest values as well as the 25th and 75th percentiles, all at the same time.

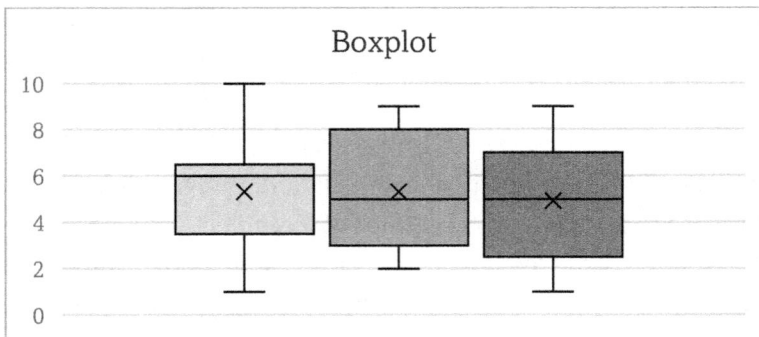

Boxplot

Prefer 100 per cent stacked bar charts over pie charts for proportions (part-to-whole comparison)

The once-loved pie chart is out of favour these days. In principle they're a good way of displaying the proportion of one category versus the others. However, the human eye is poor at estimating area in this format and you can only somewhat accurately compare slices that are adjacent. The exception is where you have limited space.

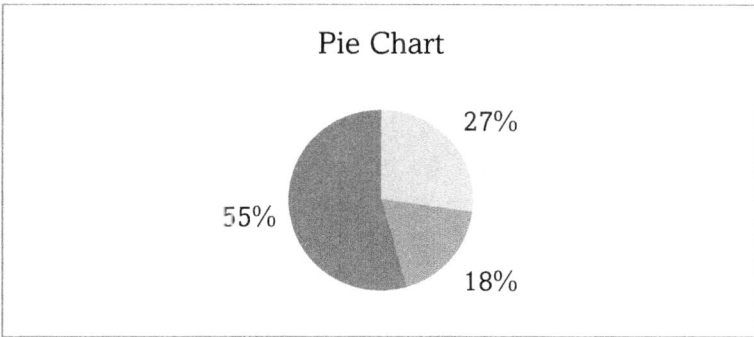

Pie charts overlay nicely on maps and – obvious as it sounds – maps are often the best way to visualise geographic information. Just bear in mind you might want to include a table alongside for more precise comparison.

Making your pie charts doughnuts instead improves the eye's ability to interpret the data, but even this format is only good for where you want to make limited comparisons – for example, NPS categories as a standalone (not multiple comparisons). If you want to compare multiple sets then it's better to switch to a 100 per cent stacked bar chart because you can look across each bar and they're easy to compare. Stacked bar charts also have limitations in terms of readability, though, when there are many categories. As the number of segments increases, they can become hard to interpret, especially when the differences in proportions are subtle.

100% Stacked Bar Chart

| 0% | 20% | 40% | 60% | 80% | 100% |

A ■ B ■ C ■ D ■ E

Word clouds are as effective as they are clichéd

A bit of an eye-roll cliché for a while, word clouds might go in and out of fashion, but they do serve a purpose: they are a great way to summarise qualitative information in an attractive and easy to understand form. Brand association words and coded thematic information work really well.

Trustworthy Personal
Premium Solid Helpful Comprehensive
Safe Confident Assured Proactive
Supportive Conscientious Expert Bold Modern
Authoritative Driven Inclusive
Commercial Agile Pragmatic Friendly Effective
Thorough Knowledgable Trust Charismatic
Personable Direct Fast Reliable Flexible
Trusted
Approachable Professional
Honest Capable Committed Competitive
Knowledgeable Economical
Dynamic

You can build in the proportion too, but this only conveys a vague sense of the variation at best – only use it where precision isn't a primary concern. The other caveat is that they don't necessarily convey sentiment. A lot of clients might mention the word 'value' but the word alone doesn't tell us the sentiment – whether they're talking about good or bad value for money.

Also consider the long list of other chart types

Tree charts, Sankey charts, waffle charts, even number tiles – there are countless others, some novelties and some with practical use. The challenge is to combine variation, which makes your stats interesting, with consistency, so that information becomes familiar and intuitive to interpret. If you have one chart where the London office is represented in blue in one chart and then, on the next page, blue is associated with spend, you're liable to confuse your audience. Similarly, it's best to reserve traffic light colours – red, amber, green – to indicate sentiment or performance outcome and not apply them elsewhere.

Finally, think twice about clever visuals that display more than one thing at once: the more complicated they are, the more likely they are to be misinterpreted or – if really overwhelming – not interpreted at all.

Data visualisation is fun. But it does require some perseverance at times and a willingness to experiment, along with a dose of intuition and attention to detail.

Create interactive dashboards for self-service reporting but limit who has access

We've talked about data visualisations – the type of charts and tables you put in reports and presentations. Dashboards are, effectively, an extension of this. They are curated sets of visualisations, but with the added dimension of being interactive. Rather than static information, your interactive dashboard console is continually updated with live data, allowing you to perform real-time data cuts, reconfigure views, and apply filters on the fly. It can be helpful to have explanatory information pop up as a 'tooltip' when hovering over it, rather than pepper your visuals with too many labels.

The beauty of doing so is that information is available on demand and so colleagues can self-serve the latest reports without the need for an analyst or other technical party.

There are, of course, dangers in putting this sort of tool in the hands of many: it can be misused, usually inadvertently. Common mistakes are simply putting a filter on a dataset so as to exclude part of the sample, forgetting about it, and consequently producing erroneous reports. These are then shared around the business, as people cut and paste them into their own materials – and here you have your inaccurate rogue reports circulating, and decision-makers drawing the wrong conclusions. It's for this reason that at many firms, even when interactive dashboards can be made widely available, they tend to limit their use to a selection of data-savvy individuals trusted to disseminate intelligence on request. In this way, you can prevent somewhat data-illiterate audiences from drawing the wrong conclusions.

Customise reports for three types of audience (frontline, management, and board)

When it comes to disseminating feedback within the firm, there are usually broadly three main audiences to share content with. The depth and nature of the insights will vary between them, as will the key messages you decide to emphasise most.

Sharing client feedback research findings widely within the firm is important because much of the problem solving needed to remedy critical issues is best captured in a crowd-sourced manner. One individual, or several, will not have solutions to every problem – the answers reside in the heads of many different individuals (depending on the nature of the problem).

The three main audiences to reach with feedback findings are the frontline, management, and board.

With the *frontline*, we're primarily talking about professionals delivering knowledge work for clients but also anyone else who interacts with clients, directly or indirectly. In terms of the insights they need, it's relatively granular and straightforward. They need to see the feedback for every client they have meaningful interaction with. It's the frontline team members who can have an immediate impact on client experience by making the quick fixes specific to each account. To be able to act, they need to receive feedback in a timely and context-sensitive manner to make improvements one client at a time.

Management is often at a disadvantage in understanding client needs and behaviours, simply because they are one place removed from day-to-day interactions. However, management also has control over and responsibility for client experience; they need to see the broader picture across each client's organisational divisions and the firm's own practices or departments. The means of addressing issues and taking corrective action is by devising process and policy improvements, by optimising investments, and providing ongoing performance management.

At the *board* level, what's most needed is an aggregate view of common issues that enables understanding of performance relative to competitors, to be able to evaluate strategic segments, and monitor overall client experience. This top-level perspective is needed in order to allocate investment and set strategic objectives that will optimise growth. Note, though, while it's important to provide aggregated information, individual examples that demonstrate wider issues are still essential. Stories bring the message to life, particularly when they're about key clients that are disproportionately important to the firm.

Benchmarking performance against your own standards and competitors for context

In interpreting results for any audience, what does eight out of 10 mean anyway? In isolation, scores are meaningless. You need reference points against which to make comparisons, to know what is poor or excellent performance. Benchmarks allow you to monitor progress relative over time against others, internally (within your firm) and externally (against others). They are key to understanding what your results mean and what action you should take with them.

The ability to benchmark is largely dependent on your structured 'quant' data, to such an extent that this should inform your criteria in selecting which questions to ask – can you benchmark the outputs?

The starting point for benchmarking is aggregated scores internally within the firm. Data can be cut in many different ways: by practice, sector, partner, teams, office, region or country, are all common ones. If the data is available and accessible, you can compare by client segments.

All these sorts of comparisons give you useful snapshots of your firm's strengths and weaknesses. That average of eight out of 10 for a particular practice or office suddenly looks marvellous when the others are averaging six, or else dire if closer to 10.

An added dimension comes when you are up and running for more than one period and can begin tracking over time. Most firms begin with annual surveys and so have year-on-year tracking. Others will progress to quarterly reporting where sufficient transactional data is being collected.

There is one word of warning on internal benchmarking to be had, where you make comparisons between departments or other types of function (known as stack-ranking results). The upside is that, by identifying those that achieve high scores, you can use their methods and techniques as a model for best practices to be implemented elsewhere – you uncover strategies and processes to target for improvement. However, when shared widely it fosters competition, which has its own pros and cons. It can drive performance improvements but, if ranking incompatible units, it will yield frustration. A team dealing with litigation, which is typically a distressed purchase with ratings closely tied to the outcome of the dispute and which unfold over longer periods are a different beast to, say, ongoing support on day-to-day employment law or from high volume real estate contracts.

From having established inward-looking benchmarking, the natural next step is to know how you stack up versus competitors. There are two means of doing this; neither is perfect but both are useful, nonetheless.

You can ask your feedback participants to rate competitors directly. You can ask them to rank other firms (score them on a 1-10, rate them as better/worse or higher/lower, and so on) against your firm.

The flaws with this approach are that, first, some people will demur from making such comparisons on the grounds of confidentiality (i.e. it's a private commercial relationship), but fewer than you might think. Second, they may bend the truth, either to save face (yours), avoiding being seemingly overly critical, or otherwise deliberately comparing you harshly in order to 'keep you on your toes'. Connected to this, a third flaw, is the inherent bias involved. Until you've got to the stage of surveying everyone, you've picked these clients because they are important to the firm and likely to be closer to you than others. Those that respond are more likely to be engaged.

It all means that, when you come to compare your firm against competitors on this basis, you'll get an overly rosy picture. At an individual account level, it's often no bad thing to confirm that a certain key client isn't about to disappear off with your main competitor but, overall, there are limits to how useful these sorts of comparisons are. You can ameliorate the bias to some extent by adding a weighting to competitor scores, factoring in your 'home team' advantage but this depends on statistical tinkering that, even when done well, only adds up to a good guestimate.

The other means of competitor benchmarking is seeking out scores from other firms. The success of this is contingent on firms using common metrics and administering surveying by similar means. The firms you are competing against most directly are unlikely to be the ones keen to share data with you. However, if you are part of a wider network of firms, a professional body, or have some sort of 'best friends' arrangement based on sharing best practices and other forms of collaboration, then these are the firms with potential for you to work with and get some perspective of your results.

If none of those are an option, you could actively reach out to other firms, but this is a time-consuming process. An alternative is to approach a research company specialising in your industry already working on behalf of multiple firms and likely to be applying a set of standardised metrics. This can be a great shortcut. You're unlikely to get a detailed breakdown but they will likely at least give you industry averages based on a basket of participating firms.

Beyond the industry specific, another useful point of reference can be comparisons with businesses from other walks of life. This can provide a tremendous reality check, because the range of performance is much greater looking when outside your own industry. Getting reference points from airlines, banks, hospitals, and so on, can be eye-opening. It can help raise your ambitions greatly if you identify a company or brand that you aspire to deliver as well as and benchmark against those levels of performance.

You can make this even more meaningful if you're able to collect this sort of information from your own clients. Working together in this way can improve those client relationships by forging a closer understanding of business drivers as well as giving you useful points of comparison. You'll interact, share, and learn from those businesses that matter most to you.

It's worth noting that the more broadly you seek out points of comparison beyond your own service specialism, price-point, or geography, the more likely you are to encounter variations owing to sector or cultural differences. You can get a false impression if you don't take this into consideration. For example: comparing a budget offering against a luxury one, relationships scores earned over extended periods versus short transactional ones, ratings that come from countries with different scoring norms than others.

Scoring can have different baselines and ranges by region. For instance, North American Net Promoter Scores typically exhibit more extremes – get it right and you get a 10, but any missteps and you'll get downgraded very low very quickly. By contrast, ratings from Asia often cluster at an upper mid-range that can be more difficult to decipher. The danger is, you end up trying to interpret national stereotypes but the reality is that norms can vary significantly between neighbouring countries.

Overall, benchmarking is an integral part of an effective client feedback programme. It's the ingredient that gives perspective on how well you are performing and where there is potential for improvement that can't be achieved when working in isolation.

Turn your research findings into actionable recommendations

Research findings are observations about the data you've gathered and interpreted, summarised in a structured form. They are the result of all that categorising and filtering of feedback. Findings are simple statements of what is happening from a client perspective.

Recommendations are an interpretation of those findings, converted into actions you suggest should be implemented. You're saying, 'Based on what you've learned, here are the actions that should be implemented'. Recommendations need to tell people what to do to improve – being merely 'interesting' is useless. Recommendations should be specific and practical. Anything vague indicates a lack of understanding or conviction. The more specific the better.

There should be a recommendation for every finding, even if it concludes that no action should be taken (because sometimes that's a reasonable outcome, when the investment isn't justified).

To arrive at appropriate recommendations, try the 'Five Whys' technique as a means of getting to root causes. It is just a series of questions but it pushes you to get to the underlying causes of any flawed client experience.

Problem
Clients complain that our professionals are slow to respond

Why?

Relationship partners are busy with many different client queries

Why?

All enquiries are triaged and then delegated by the partner

Why?

Partners own relationships and must maintain an overview of all that client's work

Why?

Belief that being first port of call strengthens relationship

Why?

Rewarded for owning relationships and billings, not whole account performance

Solution
Introduce specialists from different practices so clients can go direct while copying in relationship partner; agree acknowledgment times and add to client charter

Always share some form of 'you said, we did' summary with clients

The worst crime in the feedback world is collecting insights – taking a person's time and setting their expectations – only to do nothing. The trouble is, learning what needs to improve doesn't mean you can fix it right away. Some fixes will take months, even years. This is why you should start closing the loop by simply acknowledging the feedback received, before you necessarily have a formulated set of plans for implementation.

Those clients who need immediate action should get that at account level, but you also need a broader, shareable action plan that demonstrates to everyone that the feedback exercise was taken seriously and that, for participants, their time has contributed to some sort of outcome.

Typically, we're talking about producing a 'You Said, We Did' type of report that summarises the feedback and outlines what has been put in place as a result (or signals the plan that is going to be put in place).

Some firms get carried away, producing a huge report but doing so takes longer and, ultimately, few will read it. It's better to produce an easy to digest summary of just a few pages at most.

The 'You Said' content should be simple. It should explain what was done in the feedback exercise (who was surveyed and over what period) and summarise the common themes. Between about five and 10 is usually about right. You make it interesting by including some anonymous comments and a few eye-catching statistics. Include both the positive and negative, giving a balanced view and avoiding any extreme outliers.

The 'We Did' element summarises actions. Ideally, these should be one-for-one against the areas for improvement. The more SMART they are, the better, but obviously, not everything will apply to all clients. A small number of tangible changes are better than vague intentions.

It can be difficult to gauge what you should share because, clearly, it has to be a sanitised version of your plans that doesn't disclose anything confidential. However, if you've conducted sufficient fieldwork, it should be no problem to pick out areas that will benefit a large portion of your client base.

For large clients with multiple individuals, consider creating reports tailored specifically for those clients – it's particularly helpful for a head of department to see what his or her colleagues and direct reports think of your service; often, they don't know how valued what you do is because the more senior the individual, the further they are from the day to day.

Some of the best reports of this type are actually infographics that use lots of imagery, charts, and a few pithy quotes. Again, though, it's better to get your message out quickly while the survey or interview is fresh in participants' minds than produce something polished but long forgotten about. An email with a few bullet points is perfectly acceptable, provided the content shows the firm is paying attention and any improvements will be welcome. Doing all this helps cement client relationships by providing evidence of being a listening organisation.

Furthermore, don't limit your sharing to respondents only – distribute with as much of your client base as possible to encourage those who didn't participate this time to do so next time round. You'll even find it's good material to use with prospects – and more widely, because it underlines your credentials as a firm that listens – and one with a culture of continuous improvement.

Takeaways

- Interpreting feedback at an individual respondent level should always be your first step but aggregation of results is needed to understand wider themes, patterns, and trends in client feedback.

- Your choice of software doesn't matter much as long as you take a methodical approach, convert unstructured data into quantifiable forms, and visualise data as simply and clearly as possible.

- Even with the advent of LLM technologies, thematic coding is still an important but time-consuming task in converting data into insight – you need to allocate ample time and resource for this.

- Analysis has three stages: *stating* the evidence you've collected, *comparing* it to see what is different or stands out, and then *regression* to establish relationships or drivers of different opinions or behaviours.

- Choose data visualisations that suit your audience and your objectives. Resist anything fancy: one message per chart is best to keep things easy to understand.

- To underpin an ongoing programme, not just a one-off survey, create interactive dashboards that refresh as new data comes in. Self-service reporting is great but users must be educated to avoid misinterpretation.

- Customise reports to each audience. *Frontline* professionals need to know about account-level issues, *management* need an overview of operational matters, and the *board* need insights for strategic decision-making and resource allocation.

CHAPTER 8
CLOSING-THE-LOOP AND MANAGING CONTINUOUS IMPROVEMENT

Criticism may not be agreeable, but it is necessary. It fulfils the same function as pain in the human body. It calls attention to an unhealthy state of things.

—Winston Churchill

The only thing worse than not asking is asking then ignoring the feedback. Once you set an expectation that you'll listen and act, then there's an unwritten contract to do so. It's easy when the feedback is encouraging and the fixes are easy but oftentimes loyalty is earned when overcoming knotty issues that require great efforts internally. This is where agreed standards and set processes come in to ensure loops are closed as well as successes celebrated

Understand the emotional process of dealing with critical feedback

Feedback is wonderful when it praises, recognises your best efforts, and appreciates your time. But boy does it hurt when it's something personal, hits a nerve, or feels outright unfounded and undue. And it's easy to look at as an outsider and coach the recipient to take it on the chin, show some empathy towards the giver, or otherwise respond with stoicism or even gratitude. How different it is when it's about you! And even worse if it's being made public, without your right to reply.

It's critical that you prepare everyone for potential scenarios where they receive harsh criticism or complaints. The worst-case scenario is that the feedback recipient picks up the phone to the client and releases a tirade, refuting the client's criticism and defensively making their own case, ultimately compounding an already damaged relationship.

As much as you can try to train and prepare people in advance, it's very different when it comes along. Feedback might be a gift, but you don't always get what you hoped for. Therefore, it helps to have a buffer in place so that within your process you can step in and support the person on the receiving end. It's literally going up to them to say, 'We've had some critical feedback from one of your clients; can we sit down together to go through and put together a response plan? It may not be pleasant but it's constructive criticism, and we don't want to give a knee-jerk response.'

It could be that you need others involved too – say, a department head or the managing partner – depending on the importance of the client to the firm and the severity of the comments.

In reacting to criticism, people tend to go through three stages of emotions: denial, deflation, and acceptance.

Stage	Reaction	Emotion and Action
Denial ↓	"The client is wrong and I can prove it!"	They refuse to believe there is truth in what's been said. Their instinct may be to remonstrate with the source of the feedback. They need help regaining composure.
Deflation ↓	"I've done my best and the client doesn't appreciate it"	They start to acknowledge that – like it or not – the client's perception is also their reality. They may feel sorry for themselves and express remorse if they feel they've let down others too.
Acceptance ↓	"How do we handle this? Let's decide on the next steps"	The bitter pill has been swallowed. Now you can begin on a plan of action and how to recover the situation.

Initial *denial* is simply the belief that the other person is wrong; either mistaken or else malignly intending to undermine. They refuse to believe there is any truth in what's been said, and will not be held accountable for the state of affairs. Instead, their instinct will tend to be to lash out and remonstrate with the source of the feedback. It's important to ride this out and gain composure.

After this comes *deflation*. On reflection, they will begin to face the reality of the criticism. Although they may not initially accept blame, they will start to acknowledge that – like it or not – the person's perception is also their reality, even if it's not shared. This point can be accompanied by a great deal of negative feelings. As they recognise any failings, by commission or omission, they will start to accept blame, feel sorry for themselves, and express remorse if they feel they've let down others too.

You need to have support in place for people at this stage, to help them discuss and reflect on the situation and get them through it and onto the final stage. These first two stages take a different amount of time depending on the individual's mindset and the nature of the criticism. Some will pass through the stages in moments; others will take months.

Finally, they will reach *acceptance*. The bitter pill has been swallowed. Now you can begin to work with them on forming a plan of action and remediating the situation. There are commonly three possible routes here.

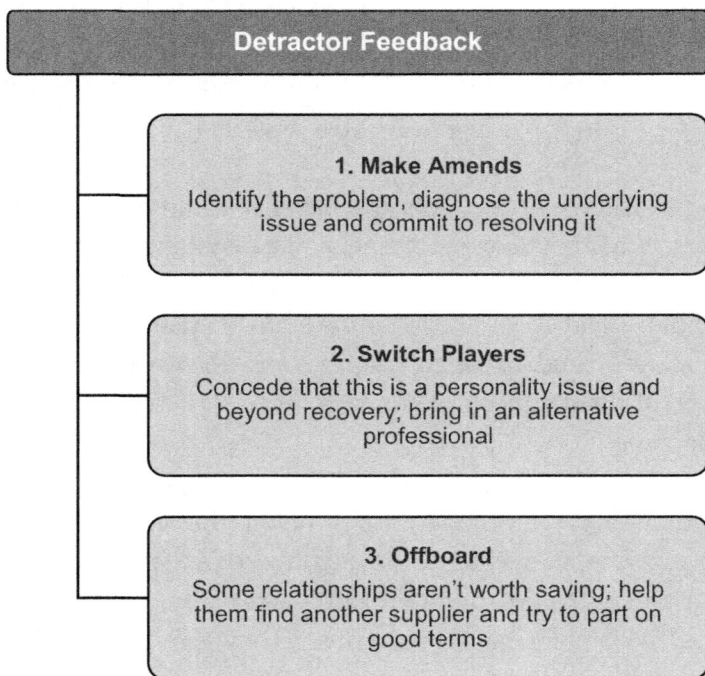

Detractor Feedback

1. Make Amends
Identify the problem, diagnose the underlying issue and commit to resolving it

2. Switch Players
Concede that this is a personality issue and beyond recovery; bring in an alternative professional

3. Offboard
Some relationships aren't worth saving; help them find another supplier and try to part on good terms

First, you form a plan and go back to the client, thanking them for their input, acknowledging shortcomings, and discussing possible fixes (you have some of your own ready, but go in with an open mind about what they think will constitute a fix). This is the approach in over 80 per cent of cases.

Second, you take the same approach but with a substitute for the feedback recipient. In some circumstances, on reflection, it may be a personality clash or a disagreement about fundamental principles that just can't be resolved but the individuals can agree to disagree and you amend the client team, bringing someone else in instead. They pick up and remediate, putting the action plan in place, acknowledging the situation and moving things on.

Third, you fire the client. No joke. Most feedback is constructive but – very occasionally – it's beyond the pale and doesn't deserve the time and effort. Sometimes it's a cry for help, asking the firm to address problems but if it's unjust or spiteful, treat it as a resignation letter. Client loyalty matters, but so does employee loyalty and they should expect leadership to have their back during difficult times. When it means sacrificing future revenues, it's never a decision to be taken lightly. Explain the decision to your client, suggest a couple of alternative suppliers that may be a better fit. Then move on, feeling the relief of pressure removed.

Most account-level responses to feedback follow a fairly simple formula: thank the respondents for their time in responding, acknowledge the points they've made, summarise your understanding (and ask for clarification if needed), set out what you'll undertake to make improvements, explaining who will do what and in what timeframe, then leave a reminder that you'll ask for feedback again in future, in order to ensure continual improvement.

This is best done as a personal follow-up, demonstrating a commitment to client experience. It's usually done one-to-one but for bigger clients it may involve a larger-scale personal presentation by the account team. It can be conveyed in email form if the contents of the client's survey responses – or the account-level of interest to the firm – don't warrant the time investment.

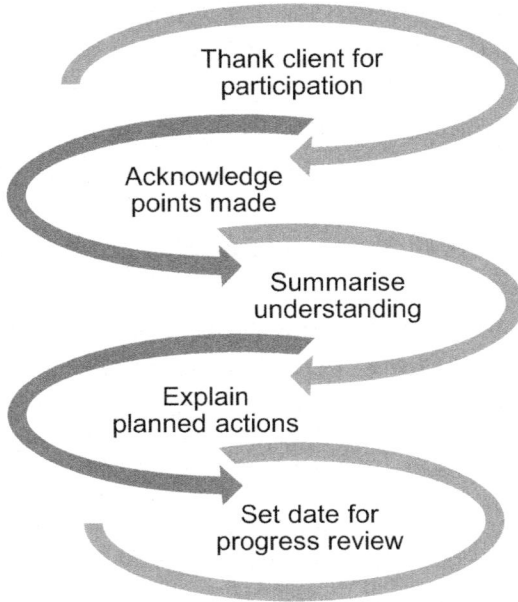

Identify, deconstruct and share the best practices from positive feedback

Thankfully, for the most part, client feedback tends to be positive and uplifting. It's encouraging and motivating to have lots of endorsements, and requires less follow-up action than when there are issues to address. But positive feedback shouldn't be filed away; it has immense value, without it necessarily being so apparent what needs to be done. It's a signal that there are best practices to be uncovered, modelled, and shared more widely.

When you see a pattern in your feedback data in which particular individuals, teams, or departments stand out, you need to recognise this and investigate further. What is it that they are doing so well that consistently has clients swooning? Sometimes the answers are there in the open-ended comments, but more often than not you need to probe for it. This is most easily done via personal interviews: a client gives a service attribute top marks, and so you literally ask:

- How is it that they've achieved that?
- Can you give me an example?
- What are they doing differently from others?

You push to get to the granular detail. If the professional receives positive scores for 'proactive communication', then what sort of comms? How often do they stay in contact? Do they call or email? What time of day? How frequently in person?

Some things are esoteric preferences that don't generalise, but other times you uncover simple little protocols that are being used to great effect, and in a pocket of the business that nobody else knows about. A data capture form that your IT director doesn't know exists (because an admin person in a department just saw the need for it and created it), maybe now smooths the client journey for that department alone and nobody knows about.

Likewise, if the answer isn't there in the feedback but clearly something is different at that particular office, you need someone on foot patrol asking what it is they are doing differently. You might need them to create, and share with you, a process diagram to compare side-by-side with different offices, or you might interview a few different people in the team to ask how they go about things. If you preface your conversation by explaining how they're outperforming everyone else, that little bit of ego boosting should help you get the insights you need!

Once best practices are identified – be they processes, techniques or technologies – they should be documented and shared. The right method will depend on the nature of the best practice – it could be via a knowledge sharing platform, publishing a case study internally, making templates available, or holding formal training on the method or techniques to be employed. The important element is that you take a systematic and collaborative approach to sharing such innovations.

Recognise that gap management is key to closing-the-loop

Beyond account-level insights, reviewing your aggregated analysis will reveal performance by various divisions – practice, office, sector, and so on – up to overall firm-wide performance. Some failings are obvious; others only emerge care of regression, or key driver analysis. It's a matter of diagnosis.

In creating a closed-loop feedback system that drives continuous improvement in the business, the main ongoing task is to identify performance gaps and decide what action, if any, to take. It refers to any element of delivery, experience, or touchpoint that falls below the success threshold you've set or else the level agreed upon with the client. Everything is relative and depends on where expectations have been set.

If a client thinks acknowledging their enquiry after a few days is good enough but you get back to them within 24 hours, you are exceeding expectations and over-delivering. If they expect responses in under a couple of hours and teams are too busy to respond, then that's under-delivery. It also makes a difference whether you have a formal service-level agreement in place or both sides are working on unvoiced assumptions about what is reasonable. The source of most satisfaction or dissatisfaction is a matter of expectation, which comes down to communication ahead of time. It's important to understand performance gap management because rather than jumping into 'fixing' delivery issues, the alternative may be to reset expectations.

Use the 'five whys' to inform account, operational, and strategic change

Deciding whether or not to introduce a service-level agreement as standard for all clients, making it part of the onboarding process, designing how it's communicated within teams, and so on, is an example of an operational improvement. It might be implemented at account-level only, or more widely across all clients. However, it's unlikely to be considered a top-level strategy decision.

Operational fixes are relatively straightforward to implement in the sense that they don't change the nature or orientation of the business. It's finding that something is not optimum in the client experience, and that the origin of the problem is in one of three areas: processes, people, or technology.

Working out which of the three is the culprit is not always easy. An apparent problem of one nature may have an entirely different source. What might first appear to be a digital user-interface problem (technology), on closer inspection may be down to human error (people), but after exploration turns out to be people following the wrong procedures (process) after all.

To get to the source of a problem, you need an iterative, interrogative approach such as the Five Whys technique in order to understand the cause-and-effect relationships underlying a particular problem. The goal is to determine the root cause of a poor experience by simply repeating the 'why?' until you can't go any deeper.

Undertaking this sort of diagnosis can rarely be done in isolation – you'll need to involve everyone with a role in delivery of the service. Doing so requires a real commitment. To some degree, it takes a fairly serious service failure to get people in the room but it is worthwhile because by doing so you can effectively crowdsource your solution: debating, honing, and going away to action what's required. The more everyone has a shared sense of ownership of the problem, the better the troubleshooting.

Given the time and resource commitment, how do you decide which areas to tackle first? Key driver analysis should have told you which factors are having the greatest impact on overall satisfaction or loyalty, so these are likely candidates. If a five per cent improvement in documentation accuracy is predicted to raise satisfaction by 15 per cent, it may look like a winner if IT tells you there's a simple cross-check of client records which will flag it.

Beyond this sort of simple cost-benefit trade-off is considering the firm's broader goals. Indeed, some questions can't be answered at the operational level; they exist in the realm of strategy. For example, if you've already exhausted possible solutions in servicing a certain type of client cost-effectively, is it that you shouldn't be servicing that particular segment of the market in the first place? It becomes a C-Suite or board-level decision.

Supply your board with a continuous stream of high quality insights

You put in all that effort getting the programme off the ground in the first place: finding champions, making the arguments, demonstrating value, winning resource, and getting commitment. Once you've started, you need to sustain the momentum of the programme by supplying insights on a continuous basis that fuel transformation and growth. Surveying brings insights that fuel change, leading to financial growth and thereby, you demonstrate value.

The key to this positive cycle is ensuring that reporting is made available to executive decision makers on a consistently regular basis. If the board sits down together quarterly, as a matter of course they'll review all the firm's key performance indicators – mostly financial metrics, along with updates on major initiatives and developments, taking them into account in forward planning.

Outputs from the feedback programme belong in the pack and you, or a colleague responsible for the programme, should make an appearance with interpretations and recommendations on a frequent basis (not necessarily every meeting, but regularly enough not to be forgotten about).

To warrant this level of involvement and sustain a flow of relevant content demands a continuous supply of insights – partly the reason for conducting not only annual relationship reviews, but more frequent post transaction surveys too. The ideal state is when execs come to expect the latest intelligence on client loyalty, service performance, competitor position, and so on, and will demand it if not supplied.

Format matters almost as much as content. The key insights should be easily digestible, easy to interpret at a glance, and in a consistent layout. A one-page summary mostly made of dashboard or infographic style information should show the headline metrics and messages (it may be the only thing that gets seen). The depth of insights should also be available in the rest of the reporting, but that front sheet or first slide in the deck ought to reveal any uncomfortable truths or revelatory news. Charts will normally have the most recent position alongside either benchmarks or previous targets for context. You should include short quotes from the open-ended questions where these support the main narrative of the feedback, especially any attention-grabbing or funny ones that provoke discussion and sharing.

Eventually, when you begin to combine financial data and client feedback, you'll have the opportunity to hybridise the two for really valuable management insight. Loyalty linked to profitability, the ability to forecast churn based on current service levels, the impact of price increases on usage.

If you have insights that call for either significant investment from an operational perspective or require a strategic decision then these are the occasions you should be in the room to frame the scenario and direct discussion. As with written forms of insight, it's best to get all the information upfront, since you never know if your meeting slot will be condensed by other agenda items.

Focus on big changes one at a time

When your feedback programme is still in its early stages but starts to achieve larger volumes, the options for change may seem overwhelming – both in terms of opportunities to pursue and problem areas to fix. However, it's hard to move the needle on any one dimension of the business, especially in larger firms, and so it's best to dedicate time and effort sequentially. Out of a dozen hot topics that arise from your research findings, which are the ones that are already recognised as strategic priorities? Which are the ones that have potential for the greatest impact? Which ones are the quickest and simplest to implement? These factors should all be considered in recommending what to pursue. Senior management will be most inclined to sign off on initiatives that are already high priority in the current business plan, if they offer relatively quick wins.

In setting the change agenda, you also need to set a time frame for achieving the outcomes, as well as the best means of measuring progress. Since most firms set targets on an annual basis, with progress towards a target monitored quarterly, this tends to be the most practical approach. The time frame will inform the degree of improvement that will be reasonable.

Ultimately, client feedback – in the form of your chosen headline metric – should gain equal weighting relative to other metrics in the firm, provided the data you collect is trustworthy, consistent, and reliable.

To set targets for improvement, you should take into account historical trend data, establishing upper and lower bounds, considering any available external benchmarks and what is realistic. In the same way that losing weight gets more difficult the more you shed, improving service performance scores gets harder the higher your baseline. Factoring in these different elements should enable you to come to a fair target at which to aim. Targets need to take into account your competitive circumstances, but setting overly ambitious targets will backfire unless you know you've unlocked the means to realistically achieving them by delivering on a plan.

Insist that client feedback be on the agenda at all conferences, AGMs, and other strategy events

While communication at board level is what gets big changes signed off and keeps the decision-makers committed to the programme, it's representation at the likes of partner conferences, AGMs, or other all-hands meetings that embeds a client-focused culture in the mindset of everyone day-to-day.

A 30-minute slot to share the voice of the client with everyone – not only those interacting directly with clients – is also key to raising the programme's profile. It reinforces the importance of client experience, explains how the programme works, and shows that each person's contribution is tracked and contributes to the firm's overall success.

Unlike board reporting, the tone of the presentation should be much more positively oriented: celebrating the successes of individuals, and the outcomes in terms of client satisfaction in the form of feel-good stories. That's not to say that you shouldn't be candid about areas of poor performance but in such cases the emphasis should be on what actions or plans are in place for improvement and how everyone can contribute to that improvement. You should galvanise everyone around a metric for improvement, with clear steps to take to move the dial by a set point in the future.

Use feedback in appraisals to motivate and inform improvement

You should definitely be using client feedback in appraisals, although not indiscriminately. It's one of the best ways to embed client focus into the cultural DNA of the firm, if everyone in the business knows that their role in service performance is taken into account.

Client feedback is a rich and detailed source of insight for use in appraisals, whether at account or wider operational level. It can be used to both inform success and to set goals going forward. It's most relevant for all those client-facing – it's most immediate when they are named in the comments. But 'back-office' functions can draw lessons too. A department head should take responsibility for their department's NPS. Similarly, a receptionist may receive feedback on how well clients are greeted and assisted upon arrival, while the head of IT can learn from the lack of complaints this year about specific client extranets or other platforms. Transactional, touchpoint surveying is particularly helpful in informing performance ratings.

Be it NPS or another headline metric that you attach to performance, for those in an account or relationship management position the other metric to monitor is participation: what percentage of the individual's clients are being invited to participate? If you're at the stage where it's mandatory to invite all clients contacts, it doesn't matter, but the earlier you are in the programme setup process, the more participation is the really critical metric. If partners are cherry-picking clients to invite, that's the more important behaviour to address and reform.

Don't link feedback and compensation (it corrupts behaviour)

There's no better way to encourage nefarious behaviour than linking remuneration and client satisfaction ratings. If you want people to beg or threaten, lie or cheat, then make their annual bonus dependent on clients giving nine instead of an eight out of 10. It's Goodhart's law that states that when a measure becomes a target, it ceases to be a good measure. Basing remuneration on client satisfaction alone completely undermines its purpose – people will game the system if it's easier than overhauling other behaviours at scale.

What works much better is making client feedback participation a component in BD performance and in turn, part of remuneration. Clients are rarely 'hidden' – they show up in CRM, marketing, and – of course – billing systems. Make fully engaging in the firm's client feedback process worth a meaningful contribution to their annual bonus and you'll see behaviours align, as though it mattered just as much as hitting billable hours targets.

Doing so sends out the message that the scores in themselves are not everything; understanding the rationale behind them is what really matters; that the firm values a feedback culture and recognises how it contributes to the success of everyone. The emphasis should be on growth mindset, not punishing those who allow their failings in client delivery to be public. Reward those who facilitate the gathering of feedback and who act on feedback in an effort to improve, not those who ensure feedback only comes from best-mate clients co-opted into singing their praises.

If you feel strongly about seeing high ratings rewarded, consider other types of reward – non-monetary ones. This is particularly good for rewarding a wider team where not every individual is directly accountable for client experience but does contribute to some degree. Non-monetary compensation might take the form of a team event or trip that not only says 'well done' but also facilitates further team-building. Likewise, featuring those who receive praise in internal communications or handing out prizes are great ways of reinforcing the right behaviour and results.

Takeaways

- Getting negative feedback can be emotional but it's also inevitable, so everyone likely to be on the receiving end should be trained in how to respond constructively and make the most of it.

- People often experience emotions of denial and deflation before acceptance. Avoid knee-jerk reactions that worsen the relationship by instead planning to either *make amends*, *switch players* or *get rid* of the client.

- Whatever the feedback, at account level, thank respondents for their time, acknowledge their points, summarise your understanding, and explain what you'll do to improve, including who will do what and by when.

- Use constructive criticism to make improvements and close the loop where under-performance exists, but also deconstruct the positives to create best practices that can be shared across teams and departments.

- Celebrate success and share positive feedback internally via multiple channels – digital and physical – to encourage a culture of feedback and continuous improvement.

- Supply the board with high quality insight on a continuous basis so that senior execs come to incorporate client insight into their decision-making as much as they do financial performance data.

- Be selective about your change agenda: focus the firm on one big change at a time and rally everyone together to make improvements that can be measured but also will make a difference to financial performance.

- Use client feedback in appraisals to motivate and inform professional development, but don't link feedback ratings to compensation because it incentivises people to game the system and ultimately corrupts behaviour.

CHAPTER 9
RESEARCH ETHICS, DATA PROTECTION AND THE MARKET RESEARCH SOCIETY CODE OF CONDUCT

We need timeless principles to steer by in running our organizations and building our personal careers. We need high standards – the ethics of excellence.

—Price Pritchett

In professional services, trust is the most valuable currency of all. It's hard-won over the long-term yet can be squandered in a second. Our research is an extension of the client relationship so is as much of a potential point of failure as any other element of service delivery. The principles of transparency and integrity are simple but their practical application requires well-coordinated collaboration and commitment.

You have a responsibility to undertake research ethically

They might be your clients but at the point at which you ask them to take part in an interview or complete a survey, they're now your research subjects too. That means some extra responsibilities when it comes to how you interact with them and what you do with information about them.

The Market Research Society is a good source of the widely accepted rules around research ethics and data handling, in line with relevant data protection laws. They address both ethical and legal matters in a very detailed way. However, while the main principles are simple in theory, they're often tricky to apply in practice. What follows is a practical guide.

Be transparent about your research purposes and how data is to be used and shared

The most fundamental principle in any research activity is that you must be clear in your purpose when asking for participation in any sort of feedback exercise. You want to be sure that clients understand the nature of the feedback you're trying to obtain and that you therefore have their informed consent. You are obliged to spell out the purpose of the study, how you're conducting it, who is behind it, and outline any potential risks or benefits it poses for the participants.

It's best to state this information in your email communications but then to reiterate the main points again at the start of the interaction, whether that's some front-end copy in your survey or a brief statement at the start of your conversation.

If you go overboard with a contract that involves the participant signing their life away, you'll scare people off. All you need is a few lines explaining that you're gathering feedback in order to improve the firm's offering and service provision, that the delivery team will get to see the feedback in order to act on it, and that – hopefully – the outcome will be a better service experience for themselves and other clients. All this need only be a short paragraph in the participation invitation, and even less in recapping again later. The main thing most people want is reassurance that their comments will only be used internally and not published elsewhere.

Don't share data for any other purpose than internal improvement

Part of this process is the need to honour the right to privacy and confidentiality. For the most part, that means using feedback within the firm and not sharing it with third parties without the participant's consent. It also includes protecting personal information and ensuring that data is stored securely, just as you would with any other client data.

The 'private' element refers to information that is personal, sensitive, or intended for a specific audience only. The 'confidential' aspect is about keeping information secret, information that, for example, must not be disclosed because it could be commercially sensitive – say, in the hands of a competitor. In other words, private information is intended for a specific audience or individual, and confidential information is intended to be kept secret.

In practice, for the vast majority of the time client feedback is not particularly sensitive or controversial. But plenty of it could cause embarrassment or offence, or be used in an untoward manner. Prime examples are criticism of individuals at the firm or, for that matter, people outside it too. Likewise, it's not uncommon to discuss business challenges and plans for the future that have implications for the firm but also for other parties, say, an upcoming merger or acquisition which may be highly privileged information and not to be divulged to the market.

Don't assume that feedback can be used as a testimonial

When you receive this sort of intelligence it's obvious that you need to deal with it in a sensitive manner. You'll have in place some of the protocols discussed already, in terms of maps dictating who gets alerted to what. The thing not to get caught out on is when you receive lofty praise that will make a perfect testimonial. You want to rush out and tell the world.

Stop.

If you haven't explicitly collected comments and ratings for that purpose, then you can't immediately launch it into the public sphere. If you pitched participation in the feedback exercise as being to help with service improvement, and gave assurances that comments would only be used internally (as a means of encouraging candid views), then clearly the use is different and you need to get permission from the source first. Although you're adding a step to the process, this isn't necessarily a bad thing. You have a reason to go and engage with the client, remind them of how much they appreciate the firm and the service they receive. Often, they'll be happy to elucidate on the praise they gave, and that one-line comment becomes a stellar case study full of texture and detail.

What's important is to see the distinction between collecting feedback and a collaborative promotional exercise, and not conflate the two. It's better to deal with testimonials as a separate follow-up exercise, usually conducted with 'promoters'.

Considering all this, you might decide you know a shortcut: simply add a data usage consent box at the end of your survey that gives permission to allow content to be shared externally. Or, you have a dedicated comments box for public sharing. Does that work? Yes. Does it ultimately compromise the overall purpose and integrity of your programme? Yes, it does. It's not good practice. And next time you ask for feedback, your client knows what you really want is for them to say nice things you can extract as soundbites that get sprayed all over your website and brochures.

Be open, honest, and accurate in your data collection

Another key element to the ethics of research is simply data accuracy: you have a responsibility to ensure that the data you collect is accurate and fairly represents the true opinions and experiences of participating clients.

In terms of sampling, it means not cherry-picking and, when surveying, not asking leading questions or trying to bias participants. You should present the whole picture to the best of your knowledge and understanding.

Essentially, don't misrepresent but also don't deceive. Well, you shouldn't *normally* deceive – but there are exceptions wherein you are allowed to withhold information to some extent, *temporarily* and only where it's necessary to the exercise. For instance, not revealing a research sponsor's name at the outset, where it might bias answers. The key thing is that you must, by the end, make a full reveal. That's an exception, and you should seek expert advice if you're running anything of that nature.

Underpinning this is ensuring that participants are not subjected to any harm or discomfort, mental or physical, during the process. Also, as already discussed, participants have a right to privacy. This means you must respect participants' privacy and avoid intruding upon their personal lives or collecting sensitive information without their consent.

Another element to consider is unconsciously biasing respondents. You should also be cautious in offering any incentives for participation. Gifts, entry to prize draws, or cash rewards, even charity donations – they must not unduly influence participant responses or compromise the validity of the data. The Market Research Society advises against using them altogether. Generally, they ought to be nice-to-have 'thank you' tidings, rather than... bribes. If a survey response or interview participation is entirely contingent on some sort of transaction, then it's at risk of influencing the feedback you're extracting. Naturally, from a research perspective, we have to avoid creating conflicts of interest that could affect objectivity or the integrity of the research being conducted. More than that, from a commercial perspective you move the focus away from relationship-building and getting genuinely constructive feedback that benefits everyone, to something transactional. Any wink-wink, nudge-nudge reason for being involved isn't good for anyone. What surprises a lot of people who move over from B2C research into B2B is how much less frequently monetary incentives are used. Where there is an ongoing business relationship, putting some time and effort into giving feedback has enough self-interest to it (with the intent of getting better service in future) that extrinsic reasons to be involved aren't needed.

One mistake to avoid is getting hamstrung by rules around unsolicited contact. Remember, this is not part of a promotional marketing campaign and therefore you're not restricted in the same way as contacting people you don't know; this exercise is an essential part of service delivery and the relationship the client has entered into with your company. You're not selling anything, and it doesn't matter if that person has or hasn't ticked a box somewhere relating to newsletters or promotional emails; this is part of doing business with your firm.

You are responsible for data protection, including encryption and storage

Besides the principle of the need to maintain privacy and confidentiality of client or research participant information, there is the practical need for data to be stored securely. Survey and interview data often contains sensitive personal information such as demographics, opinions, and behaviours that can be used to identify individual respondents. If this data is not encrypted, it can be accessed and potentially misused by unauthorised parties inside or outside the firm.

The best way to protect the data is through encryption. Encrypting survey data helps to prevent unauthorised access to the data by making it unreadable without the proper decryption keys. This ensures that only people to whom you've given authorisation have the necessary permissions to access, analyse, or extract the data.

Additionally, encrypting survey data helps to maintain the integrity of the data. Without encryption, the data could potentially be altered or manipulated – either deliberately or accidentally – by unauthorised parties, leading to unreliable or biased results. It's as basic as someone unwittingly deleting or editing files through their own incompetence in using Excel, as anything on the superspy spectrum. Encrypting the data helps to prevent these types of tampering and ensures that your results remain accurate and trustworthy.

You need to understand where – physically – software providers hold your data; in most cases it shouldn't leave the jurisdiction in which it was generated. Ensure that data is encrypted both in storage and in transit. A lot of the seemingly best software providers fall at this hurdle because they store data in countries other than your own. They make it hard to work out where their data centres are, with the spurious reason that it's for security. A good provider won't hide in which country their machines sit and will name a region, if not a specific warehouse.

It's a good idea, as part of all this, to look at your service contracts and what you've agreed with clients. Normally, it allows you to share with third parties in pursuit of delivering the service they've commissioned you to provide.

Erasing data is harder than you think – but participants have the right to be forgotten

Having covered getting permission to obtain and store data, what about when someone changes their mind? The right to be forgotten is a concept that allows anyone to request the removal of personal information generally from online sources, such as search engines or social media platforms but likewise your databases. This right is based on the idea that individuals have the right to control their own personal data and how it is used. As a concept, it's fairly new and laws vary by country.

Under the European Union's General Data Protection Regulation (GDPR), people have the right to be forgotten. That is, they can make a request that their personal data be erased by an organisation if it is no longer necessary for the purpose for which it was collected. Or simply if they change their mind and retrospectively want to withdraw their consent for the data to be processed.

This is controversial because of some implications for law enforcement, but the idea is to protect privacy and autonomy in an increasingly digital world. Beyond the legal and moral aspect, it can be a pain to implement thoroughly, especially in large organisations where data storage is not centralised and is shared ad hoc. It's easy – too easy – to ping an Excel spreadsheet with thousands of client records to a colleague who saves it who-knows-where and shares it with who-knows-who. Imagine trying to trace a single record after several years of it bouncing around between different, unconnected systems. Unless you've been careful to restrict access, it's an absolute nightmare.

There are experts out there who specialise in this process of preventing imprudent sharing, as well as the subsequent retrieval and erasure of such data. As a rough guide, though, once you've tracked it down there are three main ways that data can be destroyed:

You can 'wipe it', whereby data is permanently erased from electronic devices by overwriting it with some other random data. There are specialised software programs that do this or some devices have built-in data wiping functionality. It's more complicated to do this across whole networks.

There is digital deletion: research data can be deleted from electronic devices by using the device's built-in delete function. Literally, putting it in the recycle bin and clearing it from there. However, this method is not by any means foolproof as the data may still be recoverable using specialised software.

Finally, there is physical destruction: your research data can be physically destroyed by shredding paper documents or physically destroying electronic devices that contain the data. This can be done through methods such as incineration, crushing, or smashing the devices to smithereens. You can probably think of even more creative means but you get the idea.

The challenge with all these methods is identifying it in the first place. You need an audit trail of where the data originated and on what grounds it was collected in the first place.

Make attribution a condition of participation to avert anonymity headaches

Thankfully, it's rare that you'll get a request to remove or destroy participant data. Much more common is a request by a research participant to retain and use their feedback on an anonymous basis only. This is a right of any research participant where you are conducting a study in accordance with the Market Research Society's Code of Conduct. It does, however, throw up some practical issues you need to be aware of and prepared to deal with.

The act of anonymising data itself is straightforward enough. Where you're storing responses, usually in a database, you manually delete any personal information that could potentially identify individual respondents. Some information – like name and contact information – is obvious. You can replace names with unique identifiers, or delete identifying information altogether.

The trouble comes with small samples where you're expected to report back at an individual client level rather than at aggregate. If you have 200 interviews over the course of a year, and 20 of those asked not to be identified, you can possibly bundle them together and share those comments with the key contact information stripped out. However, people will often identify themselves through contextual references. Someone says, 'Well, as General Counsel of a FTSE-listed bank my opinion is...'. Maybe not quite so conspicuously but to that effect. Then, you end up redacting so much that there is little left to work with that's of any value. And the smaller the sample, the more impossible the task becomes.

In these circumstances you may be better to state at the outset that attribution is a condition for participation, and make explicit that you won't be able to offer anonymity. This is not ideal. But nor is this an academic exercise. It's only worth collecting feedback if you're going to act on the areas where you've fallen short. Unless you know exactly whom you've disappointed, then in many cases it's not useful intelligence.

An alternative, given the restrictiveness of offering absolute anonymity, is to have specific comments noted off-the-record. With this method, you make clear that what you discuss is going to be relayed back to the teams and individuals to which the feedback pertains, but if the interviewee wants to convey something unattributed to them you pledge to facilitate that. You make note of the comment in a separate file. It's something akin to what journalists do when interviewing politicians. They want something to be known publicly but don't want to be named as the source.

In the case of a feedback study, you maintain a file of anonymous feedback where all these blocks of comments are dropped on an ad hoc basis as you conduct your research. After a certain period of time, you accumulate enough of a quantity of these remarks that you can batch them up in a random order, stripped of any identifying information, and share that back to the business without each comment being traceable back to the originator. How long it takes will depend on the quantity of feedback you're collecting and how intensely. While the content won't be as useful as when you know who is making what complaint, at least it is not lost entirely.

Keep to the principles of ethical research, and the practical decisions are easy

There are plenty of practical challenges in being able to ensure all the ethical and security-related protections you owe to your clients as research participants. However, the principles are simple enough. You're expected to conduct your research in an honest and ethical manner, meaning you must not knowingly provide false or misleading information. You should respect the privacy and confidentiality of research participants and not disclose or use confidential information without proper permission. You need to be fair and impartial, meaning that you avoid discriminating against any individual or group. And key to all this is simply being transparent about your motives: you should always provide clear and accurate information about what it is you're trying to learn, who is involved, and how the data are going to be put to use, including who will be privy to the findings.

Takeaways

- Even if you're not a member of the Market Research Society, their guide to research ethics and practice is worth using adhering to for good data governance and research best practice.

- Be transparent about your purpose in collecting feedback: tell participants why you're asking for their input, who will get to see their feedback, and how their data will be used, stored, or transmitted.

- Feedback is more candid when you collect it on the basis that it will be confidential and used for service improvement. Therefore, don't use it for public testimonials without explicit permission.

- Be honest and accurate in what you collect and how you represent it: don't ask leading questions or try to bias participants, and think twice about how you incentivise participation.

- As well as encrypting and password-protecting data, restrict access internally to prevent any manipulation (deliberate or accidental) and remember that participants have a right to be forgotten on request.

- Decide on your approach to offering anonymity at the outset. The larger the sample, the easier it is in practical terms. However, making attribution a condition of participation is the easiest way to avoid headaches later.

CHAPTER 10
CONCLUSION: CONVERTING INSIGHT INTO PROFIT AND GOING BEYOND CLIENT FEEDBACK

The best way to predict the future is to create it.

—Peter Drucker

Client feedback still isn't embedded in most professional services firms but the trend is positive, with increasing numbers starting to get the 'voice of the client' heard at board level. As progress continues, different sources of client intelligence will converge centrally within firms, making ever greater contributions to client loyalty and profitability.

Implementing feedback is difficult but worthwhile

There's no magic formula to creating an effective and sustainable client feedback programme because firms vary so much in structure and culture. There are ingredients common to all successful programmes, though – everything described, like getting key stakeholder buy-in by establishing a financial link with success, focusing on embedding processes and feedback culture rather than immediate improvements in satisfaction scores, and relentlessly closing-the-loop to ensure that changes are implemented at both account and firm-wide level.

Ultimately, a good test of whether it's working is awareness within the firm. You should be able to walk up to anyone, regardless of their role, and ask what client feedback they're received in the last 12 months – specific to them, their team, or the firm as a whole – and they should have an answer. They should know what it *said*, what they've *done* with it, and what's *changed* as a result. Some change requires fixes but sometimes it's praise that should be celebrated – you're looking for both. Otherwise, people are operating in a vacuum, with little way of knowing if what they're doing is right or wrong.

In reality, of course, few firms can pass this test. Client experience and its measurement through feedback programmes is still a nascent discipline. Many professionals feel that their firm is behind the curve, and this sense of being behind comes from two sources. First, the software providers who promise all-in-one solutions that automate everything end-to-end want you to believe that their product will solve your problems, if only you invest. Second, since their careers depend on it, some marketing professionals are naturally keen to trumpet their successes and so they very actively publicise their incredible achievements in collecting and using feedback, glossing over all the shortcomings and failures. Combined, it's little wonder that it seems like everyone else has a better programme underpinned by better technology and greater leadership backing.

The irony of this is that if you're working in a big firm, you tend to think the small firms have an advantage because they're less encumbered by bureaucracy, have agile processes that allow quick changes, and are unlikely to be stymied by corporate naysayers. Meanwhile, those at small firms long for the infinite resources and expensive technologies available to counterparts in those long-established monolithic firms. In fact, there's no reason to feel insecure, because most professional services firms are under-supported, lack the tools, and resort to manual work-around processes. What's more important is getting underway, despite limitations, because commitment and generating initial momentum is what leads to success.

Expanding and enhancing the feedback function

What about when you do reach the stage of having implemented best practices and do, truly, have an effective programme? The next level is to make the firm's client feedback function a broader nexus for client experience. This can be achieved by integrating data from different sources within the firm. For example, by combining client opinion with service records and sales information (present in finance and CRM systems to give a 360° view of interactions). This means documenting both opinion and behaviour. The combination makes it possible to see patterns in interactions and purchasing that are otherwise hidden in siloes. Most clients have multiple touchpoints within the firm that need to be identified and monitored because it's exactly where there are blind spots, or points of overlap between departments, where the overall experience falls down. One party thinks the other is responsible and fails to communicate, or else both do and bombard the client.

To make this integration possible, the technologies under-pinning client feedback – both those that capture and which hold and display data – must be capable of interfacing with different platforms and applications. This is where it gets complicated because maintaining flexibility and agility is key; old purpose-built proprietary systems that work in isolation will no longer be fit for purpose if they cannot integrate in terms of function and data security. This is the danger with many software offerings that purport to be a one-size-fits-all solution.

In making this work – usually with the aid of cloud solutions – comes better integration with non-client data sources and operational information. For example, there's been an increase in employee surveying, driven by the desire to track well-being but also to retain talent. It makes sense to use employee perspectives interconnectedly with client views. Doing so provides a more rounded view – employee and client feedback are often two parts to the same puzzle. Problems reported by clients can often be interpreted from the point of view of those undertaking the service delivery, and from this, solutions proposed.

Likewise, non-client (or prospect) surveying tends to be undertaken separately, often as part of brand tracking, but it reveals more insight when combined with client experience. After all, they are stages in the same journey. To have a unified view of the firm, you need to bring together client, non-client, and employee perspectives.

Doing all this is what supercharges client listening, taking it from mere listening to a force for change and progress: when closing-the-loop actions are prioritised, firms deliver a differentiated experience over competitors. Business leaders who take charge of the whole client experience – not just the act of listening – will continuously modernise and adapt the firm and its services. This, in turn, leads to greater profitability and the resources to continue investment in understanding and meeting client needs.

Takeaways

- Nobody has got it cracked – even if some claim some impressive achievements – so get started and make it work on a small scale, rather than aiming for perfection from the off.

- Once you have a repeatable process for collecting feedback and generating insights, then introduce technology to combine sources, types, and channels, creating a centralised view of the firm.

- A feedback programme that helps continuously update and modernise the client experience will lead to closer relationships, increased loyalty, and greater profitability.

YOUR FEEDBACK MAKES A DIFFERENCE

Whether you are adding to an already successful programme, reinvigorating a flagging one, or starting from scratch, I hope this book has been helpful.

If there's anything I haven't covered, or you have any feedback to share or questions to ask, I'd love to hear from you – please drop me an email at graham@chorusinsight.com and I'll do my best to help.

Finally, if the information and ideas I've shared have been useful to you in any way, it would be a massive help if you could leave an honest review on Amazon, or wherever else you might have found the book. I'd really appreciate it.

ACKNOWLEDGEMENTS

Thank you to everyone who aided in the creation of this book.

I'm grateful to all those who reviewed chapters and shared insights, namely: Daniel Watt, Hamed Karimipour, Jaakko Miettinen, Jon Whiteley, Kevin Peake, Kirstie Wright, Liz Whitaker, Maria Pomoni, Nicola France, Nicola Jones, Quentin Ashby, Rob Jackson, Rose Seneviratne, and Vincent Hall. Your ideas, suggestions and support were invaluable. Thanks also to Nuno Ribeiro for his cover design.

I'm indebted to Tim Nightingale who first introduced me to client listening for professional services and encouraged me to begin conducting executive interviews.

Not a word would have been written without the understanding, encouragement and sacrifices of Alexandra Sorokina – thank you.

Printed in Great Britain
by Amazon